I Barf, Therefore I Am

A Sensitive Comedy Writer's Relationship with Cancer

Jerry Perisho

I Barf, Therefore I Am

A Sensitive Comedy Writer's Relationship with Cancer

by

Jerry Perisho

This book is designed to provide accurate information with regard to events that occurred and to the subject matter covered. This information is given with the understanding that the author is not offering any professional medical or legal advice. The author is neither a doctor, nor an attorney. Since the details of a patient's situations are all different, individuals should always seek the services of competent professionals.

Some of the names of individuals and organizations used in this book were changed to protect their privacy. The people, organizations and situations described are all real, however.

ISBN: 978-0-6152-0884-8

Dedication

To my loving family without whom I would not have
survived my fight with cancer.

Acknowledgments

I owe a very sincere debt of gratitude to the people who previewed my manuscript and freely offered suggestions to improve it. In order of their readings, they are Stephen Perisho (who read many versions and encouraged me early on), Brian Perisho (who read several versions), Christa Perisho (who read a couple of versions), Joel Perisho, Elise Smith, Jay Williams, Jan Lopez, Bill Bell, and Dwight Perry.

Additional thanks goes to Mary Davey Schambach and Bob Schambach for sharing their health insurance expertise.

And, thanks to coach and author Jim Remington for insisting that I "get off the dime" to get this book finished.

Contents

Introduction
"Vomito, ergo sum"

Philosophical I am not. But I can still hit a jump shot from 15 feet, and I am willing to bet French philosopher and mathematician Rene Descartes never could. He never blocked out for a rebound. He knew nothing about hitting an open man with an outlet pass. Actually, the game of basketball was invented 250 years after he died, but let's not obsess over the illogical.

Rene Descartes (1596-1650) has been dubbed the "Father of Modern Philosophy" thanks in part to his promotion of "rationalism", the theory that suggests "truth is not sensory, but intellectual and deductive." Rene was a party animal. Invite his crew to your New Years Eve bash and they would mesmerize your guests with their unique ability to spew reflective jargon from their croissant eaters.

The philosophical statement for which Descartes is most remembered is "Cogito, ergo sum", Latin for "I think, therefore I am." In his efforts to understand the world around him, Descartes doubted the existence of everything. But, he concluded that he existed himself, because he had the ability to doubt that very existence. Hence, his belief was that as long as he had the ability to ponder, to question, to doubt, indeed to think, then he in fact *was*. "I think, therefore I am"; this is different than the philosophical decree Popeye The Sailor espoused decades later, which he contemplatively shared with his girlfriend Olive Oyl, "I yam what I yam".

I have taken Descartes' highly respected and time-tested statement and butchered it so I can use it for my own purposes. "Vomito, ergo sum" is my own alteration to the classic dictum. (Actually, the term "Emeo", which is of Greek origin, may be the correct word to use for "I vomit", but "Vomito" just looks and sounds funnier to me.) "I vomit, therefore I am" accomplishes two distinct missions. First, it makes me smile, as I hope it does you. Just defacing a longstanding axiom with modern day insensitivities can be a great source of humor.

The second mission is the more important of the two. As a cancer survivor and patient who absorbed many infusions with chemotherapeutic drugs, I can assure you that there were countless times that I doubted whether I was going to live through the medical care, let alone the disease. It dawned on me several times over the months during which I was receiving treatments that as long as I was feeling the sting of the needles entering the veins in my arm, as long as I was staring at the ceiling in sleeplessness at all hours of the night and morning, as long as I was feeling the nausea that made me travel to the bathroom to barf, I was alive. Stated with a Descartean spin, "I was".

So, while the title of my book may have infuriated each branch in the Descartes family tree, it actually carries a very important message. It is the recognition that cancer patients often seek out normal everyday acts simply as sources of reassurance that they are still alive and still experiencing common problems. Those problems provide affirmation that the patient still "is".

I was and I am!

Poking Cancer in the Eye

"Life isn't like a box of chocolates. It's like a jar of jalapenos; you never know what's going to burn your ass."
Paul Rodriguez

There was shock on everyone's faces when I told them. A book about cancer that contains humor; what is the world coming to? You'd think I was violating something sacred. People wrinkled their brows when they heard my book idea, like I'd pinched everyone's mom on the ass, hocked up a big green loogie right in the middle of the all-American apple pie, or tricked the innocent girl next door into posing for naked Internet photos. Come on, folks. Cancer isn't sacred. It's not immune to fair and frank discussion. It's even okay if we make fun of it. Cancer is not something that belongs up on a pedestal. It's a terrorist and we should be doing everything we can to expose it for what it is, and to beat it out of our lives. We should treat cancer with extreme caution, but not with reverence, and we should not cower in fear. We need to rise up and knock the chip off cancer's shoulder. We should not be gently and respectfully handling it with kid gloves like it deserves the key to the city; we should be manhandling it with pick axes and blow torches and we should spit in its eye and defiantly tell it we hate it.

Granted, cancer is a nasty, son-of-a-bitch disease that comes in too many forms to describe. It hurts and kills millions of people every year. It is a non-discriminating disease that attacks both men and women. It has no regard for race, religious beliefs or sexual orientation. It doesn't care when you were born or where you live. It doesn't care who you know or how much money you have. Cancer is a heartless bully. And there is nothing innately funny about having it.

Prostate cancer is an especially devious twist on the disease that attacks men in their reproductive and urinary parts. That's what I've got: prostate cancer. If the fear of having the disease doesn't piss you off, the surgery and its long-lasting aftereffects most certainly will. Historically, prostate surgery, a "radical prostatectomy" for all you medical terminology buffs, is an operation that has left its male patients unable to achieve erections, unable to control their flow of urine, with a recovery period that would keep them off work for many weeks and with absolutely no guarantees that the cancer wouldn't kill them anyway. Other than that, having prostate cancer is a cakewalk, a stroll in the park, a night at the opera. So, what prompts a funny book about the combination of cancer and surgery, incontinence and impotence, and let's not forget chemotherapy and hormone therapy, and maybe someday radiation and death?

The hope and healing that laughter and a positive attitude bring to the fight against illness are the genesis of this book. The truth is... a diagnosis of cancer is not a death sentence. Let me say it one more time, this time in italics because that's one of the ways you indicate emphasis when you're writing a book... *being told you have cancer is not the same thing as being told you're about to die.* More people are beating cancer today than ever before. In the vast majority of cases there is reason to have hope; hope for a cure, hope for an extended life full of joy, hope for fulfilling experiences with your loved ones. Whether you have surgery, radiation, chemotherapy or weird combinations of all three, there is still time to be capitalized upon. Measured in years, months, days or hours, we have to seize the opportunities that time offers. There are hugs to be shared, as well as tears. There are lessons to be learned, as well as taught. There is love to be delivered, and received. There are still jokes to be told and belly laughs to enjoy.

I want you to laugh. Laugh about the stuff that has happened to me and about the funny things that are happening to you. Recognize the hysterical uniqueness in the people you meet and the things they say and do. Laugh out loud. Luckily, laughter is good for you. Somewhere in your life you have learned about author Norman Cousins' landmark book *Anatomy of an Illness as Perceived by the Patient*. Decades ago, Cousins theorized and then later proved that laughter can help the body to produce its own painkilling and healing medications. It seems completely logical, doesn't it? Think about how good it feels to you every time you're doubled over with laughter. Well, there is medical evidence that all that chuckling, cackling and howling actually does you good. Today, researchers tell us that laughter has a positive effect on your respiratory system, your cardiovascular system, your muscular system, your central nervous system, your endocrine system, your immune system, and even your computer system. Nah, I was just kidding on that last one. Having confirmed Cousins' suppositions, medical experts today are actively practicing "laughter medicine" in hospitals around the country. They offer funny videos and produce skits and plays that help their patients to laugh and to temporarily escape the pain they're in.

Of course, it is not reasonable for someone with cancer, nor for those living with cancer in a loved one, to laugh all the time. Your goal should be that you identify the things that make you happy and that you not forget how to laugh at least occasionally. Even though you or a loved one is ill, the challenge is to create a healthy balance of activities in life. It is easy to become so mired in the fear of dying that you forget how to enjoy living. I want this book to help you prevent that from happening.

A few months after I began recognizing that many unexpectedly strange and humorous episodes were happening to me during my battle with cancer, I told friends I felt the curious need to write an account of the extraordinarily fascinating people and events and interactions I was experiencing. Doubting the wisdom of such an undertaking, I asked my surgeon, Dr. Timothy Wilson and my oncologist, Dr. Przemyslaw Twardowski, both practicing medicine at City of Hope National Medical Center in Duarte, CA, if there was "room for comedy in the world of cancer." I did not know then how humor might fit into the treatment of disease; I did not know how medical professionals would feel about my desires. Without hesitation, they assured me there was plenty of room for humor in their fields of expertise and they encouraged me to write. They convinced me that the world of cancer needed an upbeat, slightly irreverent perspective and that I was the man to communicate it.

Early considerations of this book were pop-up editions. You know those amazing kids books that open up to reveal three-dimensional depictions of the Washington Monument or the Eiffel Tower or the Sears building in Chicago with King Kong swatting at circling biplanes? Well, that same breathtaking pop-up book-making technology could be used to provide a three-dimensional look at the male anatomy. Turn a page and the reader could witness a 1:1 scale model of the human male erection. (Publisher's note: the uncircumcised version of the book would cost just a bit more for extra materials.) Turn the page to see the pop-up version of the normal sized prostate. Not too impressive, huh? But, stand back and turn the next page; wow, look at the enormity of the engorged, swollen melon-like features of the enlarged prostate. It leaps right off the page at you. Go ahead and tap it; see how hard it is? Notice its unhealthy murky brown color. (Publishers note: Please use either Pantone #117 or #1255 to fully capture the grossness.) *Isn't it enormous? Look at how it pinches off the urethra so its owner can't urinate very well. I'll bet he has to make lots of trips to the bathroom every night.*

I was even willing to unveil my very own new invention. This is something that has not been introduced into the book-making art, as of yet; it is called "inflatable literary technology". Here is how it would work in my pop-up book: to start, try picturing the life vest the FAA makes your flight attendant demonstrate in front of a plane full of disinterested passengers. A firm tug on the red handle, or you can blow into the inflation tube, and two human-sized balloon-like butt cheeks would appear right before your eyes. Just slip on the rubber glove that was included with the cost of the book, dab on a bit of lubricating jelly, or I Can't Believe It's Not Butter, just like a real doctor does, slip a digit into the rubberized rectum where the flashing yellow arrow is pointing, and the reader gets to conduct a realistic prostate massage. Touch the battery-operated button that lies deep inside [Publisher's note: naturally batteries are not included in the price of the book] representing the sought-after prostate gland and the small speaker imbedded in the pages emits a disquieting human grunt, just like the one a live male patient would make.

It all sounded like fun, but I just didn't think it would sell in middle America, and I did not know how much it would help those going through difficult times. As I started creating the book you're reading, which has no three-dimensional pop-up pages, I knew I did not want to regurgitate to you the complex details of human anatomy, how cancer is affecting your metabolism and precisely what the survival rates look like. This book won't talk about how cells are multiplying out of control, and it won't go into specifics about therapies or surgical procedures or the latest double-blind studies. There are plenty of those publications available. I read many of those books and documents before deciding my own course of treatment. Don't be afraid to buy them. In fact, you need to read them for your ongoing education. You must be informed so you can beat the disease.

You'll find those other publications in the medical-reference aisles in the bookstore. You may have found this book sitting alone on a shelf labeled, "We Don't Know What Genre This Belongs To." My hope is that this book will keep you headed in the right direction and keep you moving toward getting well and help make you smile. This is the "gutter bumper" of cancer books; you know, those inflatable cushions that bowling alley operators put in the lane-side troughs when the really crummy bowlers are launching balls at the pins. Their purpose is simply to keep the ball rolling in the right direction so nothing gets damaged while neighboring bowlers are having fun. Yes, I have included some stories of incidents that made me burst out laughing on my own journey. And, I am including some jokes to help relieve the pain you may be feeling. But, it is important that you, as a cancer patient or the loved one of a cancer patient (or simply as a human being trying to stay well), keep moving forward. Do not allow the fear of cancer to paralyze you. Remaining motionless allows cancer to win without a fight. This is the worst thing we can do.

I have learned a great deal about how a patient under stress can manage his actions and interactions to get the most out of his disease-fighting efforts. I have learned that sick people scare the crap out of their family, friends and co-workers because each of them is already living his own fragile life and they just do not know what to say to you when you are the sick guy. I have learned that by gently pushing on and prodding certain parts of the medical and insurance systems, and by screaming at others, the patient can get close to 100 percent of what he wants, needs and deserves. You will read about the way I dealt with all of those medical realities and hopefully laugh along the way.

I am a comedy writer at heart, I have been all my life, and I was fortunate enough to start a small business and make some good money writing jokes. I have always tended to look at life through the lenses of cynicism and lampooning and rancor. Where many people weep, I sometimes chuckle. An avid TV buff all my life, I closely identify with the episode of the legendary *Mary Tyler Moore Show* where the WJM-TV news crew attended the funeral for former on-air kiddie show host Chuckles the Clown. The storyline tells us that Chuckles

13

had met his demise when he went to a circus parade dressed as Peter Peanut. There, a rogue elephant tried to shell him. You may recall that Mary Richards struggled not to laugh during the funeral proceedings. As those who knew him settled down for the eulogy, they listened to the minister quietly and respectfully share one of Chuckles' personal mottoes, the so-called credo of the clown, "A little song, a little dance, a little seltzer down your pants," and Mary burst out laughing. She struggled not to be disrespectful, but she saw the incongruity of the moment and she could not control herself.

That is the way I have lived much of my life. I seem to identify absurdities in the everyday moments I am living, and that ability has gotten me in deep trouble more than once. I have always been distracted by the underlying humor in situations, even when only a shred exists. During the years I was a senior vice president of a small company in southern California, senior officers' meetings were designed to provide serious reviews of corporate operations and elicit meaningful discussions of the organization's future. While the weekly gatherings appeared to be dead serious to most of the other eight people in the room, the sessions were frequently, in my view, little more than exercises in stroking egos and wrestling for power. As I watched those in the meeting lock horns in an attempt to mark their territories and stake their claims, I often fidgeted and fussed, coughed and cleared my throat just to keep from howling with laughter. Making eye contact with another person who also saw the meeting for what it really was, on more than one occasion, caused that colleague to break the quiet in the room with an unprofessional snort of concealed laughter or a spewing of coffee onto the boardroom table. I will share with you the way that this admittedly peculiar attitude has positively affected my battle with cancer, beginning the day I learned of my diagnosis.

Today, I have a very personal relationship with prostate cancer. I have not beaten it. In truth, I don't know for certain that I am even close to victory. For now, cancer is crouched over there in the weeds, maybe waiting to pounce on me again. I can see it peeking at me from the shadows. We do not have any kind of understanding or agreement, cancer and me. Cancer and I do not see things eye-to-eye. We do not relax together in the evening and buy each other drinks. I hate this disease and by its very nature it acts like it hates me. In fact, it wants me dead. I am battling it as I write these words with the medications I take every day, with good nutrition, with regular exercise and with a very positive attitude, and I will continue to do everything I can to beat it. So, please do not mistake my cynicism, my sense of humor, for cockiness or uncaring or naiveté. I am not arrogant and I am not overconfident. And I am neither ignorant nor misinformed. Cancer is an evil, unfair and potentially deadly parasitic opponent that looks for weaknesses in its host and works to strangle the life out of it. I am just doing my best to defeat it, or at the very least to extend the engagement for a long time, to give cancer a run for its money and to enjoy my life. I encourage you to do the same.

Cancer is very much a reality in my life, so around my house I started calling myself "Cancer Boy". It's a self-deprecating term that brings cancer out into the open and does not let it hide in the recesses of people's emotional blind spots. My wife took to the moniker pretty quickly, but each of my three sons and my daughter-in-law struggled a bit with employing this form of black humor. Each of them had to take a first shot at using the term and getting comfortable with it, but now it is thrown around fairly freely: "*Everybody else wants extra cheese on their pizza; somebody shout at Cancer Boy and find out what his sorry ass wants.*" I have given everyone within earshot of me permission to mock the disease this way. It makes me laugh when I hear my family and friends thumb their noses at cancer. I do not take the nickname "Cancer Boy" as a personal offense. Just the opposite, the name gives me power over the dreadful disease. I wear it as a badge of honor. We are not being brash. It is simply a way to cope and it is a way to keep the disease from secretly dominating my every subconscious thought and action. And

I most sincerely look forward to the day that the label "Cancer Boy" will be replaced with the proud and distinguished label "Cancer Survivor".

Join me as I recount my journey through the ongoing battle with prostate cancer. Take the lessons Cancer Boy has learned and apply them to your own fight. I think laughing is a good thing to do when you are sick; so is crying. I encourage you to do both.

Ain't Nothing Positive About These Results

"Waiters and waitresses are becoming much nicer and more caring. I used to pay my check, they'd say, 'Thank you.' That graduated into 'Have a nice day.' That's now escalated into 'Take care of yourself, now.' The other day I paid my check; the waiter said, 'Don't put off that mammogram'."
Rita Rudner

Some people would call me hypocritical, untrue to myself, or maybe just a big crybaby. Others would protest, "He's exhibiting bad sportsmanship" and demand a level playing field. I prefer to think of myself as curiously complex. All my life, I have loved creating convoluted surprises that put people on the spot, forcing them to break into just a bit of a sweat. If there is a roast to celebrate an anniversary or a retirement, a comedic parody of someone's life or just a simple party that will leave one of my friends or family members wide-eyed, open-mouthed and in shock, then count me in. I remember a couple of decades ago when my sister-in-law Lois phoned me with the news that she was planning a surprise 40th birthday party for my brother Joel and she wanted me to participate along with a group of his friends in paying homage to his advancing age. I remembered the old 35-millimeter home movies from the 1950s that my parents had pawned off on me because they were taking up space in their garage, although my dad had absolutely nothing of value to fill the newly emptied space. I got them out and used them to help roast the heck out of the guy. My wife and I appeared, along with a dozen other out-of-town guests and friends, much to his bewilderment. It was fun; he was shocked, but he gathered his wits and defended himself admirably. Well, don't ever do that to me. I hate having surprises sprung on me. Hence, the curious complexity of one Jerrold Perisho.

You never know when something is going to sneak up on you and bite you on the ass, though. How about the fight-or-flight feeling you get when you're walking alone along a lovely wooded trail and you hear creatures skittering in the bushes nearby? You start to whistle or hum or even act like you're talking to the other dozen people you suddenly wish were with you. Your mind wants to believe it's just a lizard or a rabbit or a blue jay rustling some leaves, but the adrenaline that has started coursing through your veins is telling you to be prepared to do battle with a truly frightening beast like Big Foot or a grizzly or the entire East German women's weight-lifting team. East Germany no longer exists, let alone its women's weight-lifting team, but remember how scary they were? Usually, it's nothing more than the wind.

Regardless of how much you despise surprises, the world of medicine is full of them. A sore throat becomes tonsillitis and boom, "Surprise!"; before you have a chance to croak "I'm starting to feel a lot better," a snarling doctor with an enormous house payment, an enormous ego and grotesquely enormous sausage-like fingers is reaching down your throat with some rusty pliers and yanking your tonsils out. *Now, wasn't that fun? Here, eat your body weight in ice cream, kid.*

Anyone who has ever had a tissue biopsy knows what it is like to count down the days to hear the results of the tests, hoping not to be surprised with bad news. As I was about to leave the doctor's office on prostate-tissue-sample-donation day, the nurse muttered, "OK, Mr. Perisho, we'll have those biopsy results back from the lab one week from today." A week? I could not believe it was going to take them a full week to tell me whether or not I had cancer. *Don't they understand how important this is to me? Can't they shove all those other slides aside and put these at the top of the pile? That's what I get for belonging to an HMO that uses Wally's Discount Grout Repair and Pathology Lab. Anything to save a couple of bucks!*

"Come to Wally's: Quality Tile Grouting and Lab Services Since Last April".

A prostate biopsy is a procedure that Mother Nature intended never be performed. She cleverly and quite intentionally placed the man's prostate in such a delicate and protected location in the middle of his pelvic region that a digital examination of the gland alone is offensive and humiliating to many, to say nothing of trying to dive in there and grab little pieces of it to examine under a microscope. Core samples; they actually called these little nuggets of tissue that are soon to be selected and dissected and resected and inspected... core samples. The whole experience was kind of like a diamond miner heading deep into a rock quarry, a shaft that I had freshly douched with an at-home self-administered Fleets enema, just hours earlier. To obtain these core samples, the urologist initiates something called a transrectal ultrasound-guided needle biopsy procedure. You've probably seen this device before... at the House of Wax where the mannequins are seen torturing one another. He starts off by pulling on his spelunker's helmet with a big 50,000-candle power light focused directly on your anus. He slips his hands into some heavy work gloves and pulls the oxygen mask down over his face. The canary in the cage beside your gurney will immediately tell him if he's hit a deadly pocket of gas. Then, while you are lying on your side and wondering

22

what the hell is about to happen to you, he inserts a device up your butt that has about the girth of a finger, but feels bigger than a canned ham; I've never actually had a canned ham up my butt, but one can only imagine. Next, Doctor Hurtsalot fires off a series of spring-loaded needle attacks on the gland that peacefully resides in the middle of your body where it thought it was safe. The needle pierces the rectum wall and enters the prostate gland. Each time this hollow weapon of Satan fires, it grabs a little tubule of prostate tissue and yanks it back out. That little tubule is the core sample.

This was the feeling that one uses to describe how painful other things feel. Like, if you bite down on a piece of ice with a new filling in your tooth and feel that terrible sensation travel up one of your nerves, you might describe the pain as, "It felt like a hollow needle piercing my rectal wall and entering an internal organ." Well, this prostate biopsy WAS a needle piercing an internal organ… repeatedly. The entire episode lasted about 20 minutes; it seemed like 20 hours. I had six core samples taken that day and was soaked in sweat when I was done.

Nearly a week later, I walked in the front door of my home in Whittier, CA after working all day for The Company With No Soul. The large interstate corporation that had acquired the smaller local company where I was happily employed as a senior vice president was not really The

23

Company With No Soul, but that is the name I have assigned it in this book because the decision-makers there did not care at all about our employees, the firm's customers or good decision-making practices. Their home offices were located outside of the state of California. Let's just say they were the only game in town where they were founded, and they knew nothing about the local customer service environment. In their stronghold, they thought they were corporate geniuses, so they did not give a squat about any special service nuances particular to far-off Southern California. Hence they became The Company With No Soul. I have assigned the small community-based organization that had just been purchased the tender, heartwarming moniker, TLC Inc.

When I entered the house that Thursday afternoon, the phone was ringing. I consciously reminded myself that the biopsy results were not due until tomorrow. Still, that tiny unnamed voice inside my head (many of the other voices in my head have actually told me their names) suspected that it was my urologist on the line and that he wasn't calling me after 5 o'clock that afternoon to excitedly talk about the latest Dodgers debacle. I didn't even get a chance to put down my briefcase, the faux leather weapon of the modern-day businessman, before clicking the talk button on the cordless phone. "Hello", I said with my usual flair and colorful control of the English language. When I heard the doctor's voice on the line, I longed for him to proclaim, "Jerry, we just got your test results back from Wally's Discount Grout Repair and Pathology Lab and not only are you cancer-free, but the nurses here have unanimously voted you the healthiest, studliest specimen of a man who has ever strolled through our office doors." He missed by a mile.

It's dangerous telling someone he has cancer when he's holding his fake leather briefcase. The thing must weigh 50 pounds. It's full of all sorts of important stuff. Stuff that could easily, in a moment of sheer terror, be slung against the family room wall, only to break picture frames and centuries-old heirlooms and scare the hell out of the cat. In the blink of an eye, the air could be filled with rocketed mementos of meaningless business meetings and lots of free crap from the company supply cabinet. If you're not careful, your 10-year horde of Acco paper clips could end up scattered across the recently-polished tile floor. That might have happened in my house that day if we'd had any heirlooms. That and the fact I didn't have the energy to sling the briefcase. It suddenly weighed a thousand pounds, and I barely had the strength to remain standing, let alone to sling anything.

Nope, when he called and talked to me in his very calm voice, I stood there in shock. Hearing that you have cancer is a horrifying, terrible, hideous moment in your life. There is finality in hearing that news. No longer can you

25

think to yourself "Sure, I might have cancer some day, but I don't want to think about it." Instead, the moment is here and there is no turning back. It's not a matter of whether or not you want to think about it; the challenge is to think about anything else. Sadly, as much as you would like to, you cannot unring that cancer bell.

I had never before heard 10,000 radios playing in my head all at the same time, but that is the way I felt at that moment; that is what I heard. I was standing in the doorway, the front door still open. Outside, I am sure the birds were singing in the trees and a gentle wind was blowing, but inside my head was nothing but noise. I was paralyzed with a kind of sensory overload as the synapses in my brain attempted to fire once again in a rational sequence, but failed, and my heart tried to control the sudden rise in blood pressure that produced the lightheadedness. Time stopped as I hit the alt-ctrl-del sequence and tried to reboot my brain.

Christa, my beautiful wife of 31 years and the person who was about to assume by default the role of "Jerry's designated urine bag emptier" and who had watched the blood drain from my face as I listened to the voice on the phone, hugged me. Once the noise cleared my mind I cursed Alexander Graham Bell for having ever invented the telephone.

My urologist, Dr. Gregory Polito, had received the lab results and they were positive. They were *positive?* I have trouble with that! I mean, of course I had trouble with finding out that I had cancer; wouldn't you? But, why are **positive** medical test results filled with nothing but lousy news? Why does the medical profession have to call them positive? Why aren't medical tests that show you had a heart attack or that you've got cancer or that your vasectomy grew back called "negative"? That's all bad news. I like positive stuff!

"Jerry, we're going to offer you the new job and we're going to pay you an incredible amount of money."

"Are you sure I am the best candidate and the most highly qualified comedy writer to join your staff, Mr. Leno?"

"Yes, we're positive!"

You see? Now, that is good news! Listen up, medical profession, and take notes.

"We've got your biopsy results, and they are positive," Greg said after a moment's meaningless chit-chat. "What does that really mean, Doc?" I asked in a desperate attempt to sound calm, eloquent and inquisitive, knowing full well what it meant, but I needed to hear him clearly and concisely state it, so I knew that the sudden urge to projectile vomit was truly justified. He did. They found cancer cells in the prostate tissue I had unhappily donated a week earlier. Two of the six core samples. It meant I had prostate cancer.

Greg is a good friend, and he was very supportive. I'm guessing this wasn't the first time he had heard such a stunned response on the other end of the line. He made special arrangements to consult with Christa and me at 9 o'clock the following morning in his office. He said it was "to review our options." *We're going to consult about "options"? Dammit, I don't want to have to discuss options on anything but maturing bank notes or maybe a lucrative power forward contract with the Lakers.* We made plans to meet in his office the next day.

I stood there. The phone in one hand and my briefcase full of important businessman stuff that didn't mean a damned thing in the other, I stood there. Then I hung up the phone and I began apologizing to my wife.

It was not something that I had planned. I had never thought about what we would discuss if I were to receive this phone call. Nature took over, and I apologized to her for being such a flawed human being. Like I needed some social misfit in a pathology lab with his eye glued to a microscope to enlighten me that I had flaws; ha! But, this time I was flawed big. This was not some little behavioral problem like forgetting my locker combination or not throwing my dirty socks in the clothes hamper. This was the big one. This was

28

cancer. This was prostate cancer and this little imperfection was going to kick my ass. Or so I feared.

We lay on the bed together and hung on to one another and cried as I asked my wife to forgive me for the pain and the unhappiness and the disruption that I was about to put us both through. I told her that I was sorry I was going to change our wonderful lives so horrifically. In return, I got the steadiest stream of reassurance that a man could ever hope for. Christa promised me that I wasn't flawed and she guaranteed that everything would be all right. We both knew that she couldn't accurately predict that I would beat cancer and be cured, but she was promising to be there for the battle. I knew her guarantee was heartfelt and the words were exactly what I needed at that terrifying moment. And then we went to the refrigerator and each ate a half-gallon of Swiss almond vanilla ice cream. When we were finished, I still had cancer, dammit.

We cried a lot together in that first hour of our new and unwanted association with cancer. We were feeling what every family confronted with this bastard of a disease feels. First, we were afraid I was going to die a slow, miserable, painful death at a young age; I was 52. And if it wasn't Death whispering in our ears with its putrid breath and heartless raspy voice, then it may have been Death's mongrel back-woods, in-bred cousins, Pain and Illness. Pain specializes in

29

the invasion of tender tissue and celebrates when we are forced to curl up into a ball to avoid its terrible effects. Illness loves to watch us wither away as it forces us to miss meals and lose precious body weight. These sick sons of bitches had somehow wormed their way into our lives, and we were not yet sure how to deal with them.

There are so many things I wanted to do in my life, so many things I wanted to see. I wanted the chance to witness all three of my sons getting married. I wanted to follow through on the promise I made to my Grandma Thayer decades ago, when on her 65th birthday she danced the twist to Chubby Checker music with her grandchildren and made us all promise to do the same on our 65th with our own grandkids. For crying out loud, I just wanted the chance to meet my grandkids and to let them crawl into my lap and feel the love I felt as a young boy when I was securely nestled in my grandparents' laps. All of the personal dreams I had for the latter part of my life were crashing and shattering into millions of pieces.

We had to think about the next morning's meeting with the urologist and began figuring out how we would make the time to be there. Fortunately, I had accumulated a large amount of sick time at The Company With No Soul, allowing me to take time off at my own discretion. I had no trouble making arrangements to take the next day to visit

Greg's office. A couple of quick phone calls cleared my calendar. And hey, I had cancer; if The Company With No Soul didn't like me being gone one day, then let them fire my malignant ass! After all, I had already stolen my 10-year supply of paper clips.

We both knew Christa should be with me for the "options" discussion with the urologist. Christa is a first grade teacher. She is a great teacher! When her kids enter her classroom at the start of a school year, most of them don't know how to read or write or add or subtract. Some of them don't even know how to blow their nose or go to the bathroom alone. Over the summer, they've forgotten the social skills they learned in kindergarten, like how to stand in a straight line without punching the next kid in the head. But when they're done with their school year in her classroom, her students are ready to move on. They have learned how to solve problems, how to respect one another and themselves, and how to make good decisions. If only we could get members of Congress to spend a year in Christa's first grade classroom our country would be far better managed. Actually, Washington, D.C., is a lot like elementary school, except Christa's first graders aren't nearly as whiny and vindictive.

She had to figure out how to get lesson plans for the next day to her school so a substitute teacher would be

31

properly prepared. She hurriedly jumped onto the computer and put some materials together for her sub, but then struggled with how she was going to deliver the plans to school. She called our good friend and fellow teacher Pam Thomas to share our horrible medical news and to ask for her assistance. Pam agreed to come by our house that evening to pick up the lesson plans. Two hours after receiving the terrible "your tests are positive" call from Dr. Polito, our close friends Pam and Lane Thomas were trudging up the steps in front of our house to knock on our front door. Their eyes were red from crying, their gut-check reaction to my having cancer.

The Thomases did not hesitate to wrap us in their arms to comfort us. They did not question whether it was the proper thing to do. They were not concerned that they might be uncomfortable visiting their friend who has cancer; they knew it was right. They were in pain, and they came anyway. They walked in with tears rolling down their cheeks and they shared their love, their heartbreak and their shock. And they allowed us to share ours. We all talked openly about our new fears; our fears that cancer might invade all of our lives.

Pam Thomas is one of the kindest people you could ever know. She cares about children and small animals and the hungry and the poor. She raises beautiful flowers in her garden at home, and she loves God. She is a wonderful mother of three grown children. Lucky for me, she cares about her friends, too. After an hour spent consoling two such friends who just learned that cancer had arrived, Pam was emotionally spent. She was tired and wanted to go home. With all of the genuine sincerity a person can possess and with all of the composure she could muster at the moment, Pam looked me in the eye and offered, "Jerry, if there is anything either Lane or I can do for you, please don't hesitate to ask. We'll do anything."

That is when it first hit me. *I have cancer; I feel like shit; this is very serious; and still, I have the incredible desire to make a joke and have a good laugh.* Researchers have attempted to measure the speed by which the human brain computes. They believe it takes 250 to 300 milliseconds, about one-quarter of a second, for the brain to begin to recognize an object or concept, and another 250 to 450 milliseconds to fully comprehend it. So I figure it took me less than a second to debate the appropriateness of the joke that was about to fly out of my mouth.

Is this the right moment to make light of a serious situation? Where is this joke coming from? Would making a joke at this moment show unbelievably poor taste? Screw it! I have cancer. Who's gonna call me on it tonight? Even if it's not funny, maybe they'll laugh out of pity for me. Go for it, baby. Let 'er fly!

Every prostate patient, let alone every man over the age of 50, has had a doctor feel around for an enlarged prostate gland. You bend over an examination table while the doctor sticks a lubricated gloved finger in your butt hole to feel for anything unusual, any irregularities of the gland, which is nestled against the rectum. This digital exam is completed very quickly and without pain. Still, this unwelcome and seemingly unnatural act is the fodder for millions of jokes: *Why does my urologist sit back and smoke a cigarette when he's done with my prostate exam? Does every doctor turn off the lights, warmly illuminate the room with scented candles, and then hum "Sometimes when we touch, the honesty's too much"? My doctor uses hand puppets for my prostate exam; is that wrong?*

After 750 milliseconds of agonizing internal debate, I did it. I fired off the first joke of my post-cancer-disclosure career. And, it felt good... damn good. In response to her generous offer to do anything I might need, I said to Pam, "Well, there is one thing that would help me feel a lot better right now."

"What's that, Jerry?"

Showing at least a crumb of decorum and trying to save Pam just a bit of personal embarrassment by not making her the target of the disgusting plea I was about to offer, I feigned sincerity and quietly muttered, "I'd really like Lane to give me a prostate massage, right now."

34

It wasn't the creativeness of the joke that was key; in fact there was nothing creative about it. No, the crux of the joke's success at this moment was its timing. Remember, I'm the guy who likes to surprise people, but hates getting surprised back. These two poor innocents, my very dear friends, the people who had sucked it up to come over to visit "Cancer Boy" in those first tender hours, did not know what to do. Dead silence! Not only did they come to my house under deplorable conditions for the sole purpose of offering comfort, I decided to throw them the ultimate curve ball. Christa eyed me and telepathically said, "You didn't really do that, did you?" She would have called me a jerk, too, but she remembered, "Hey, the guy's got cancer; screw it."

The mental deliberation that I had tackled just moments earlier had been rather unexpectedly lobbed to the Thomases like a hot lug nut. Do they laugh? Should they express pity for this poor disease-addled mind and soul? *Could he possibly be serious? Is this guy really that big of an asshole?*

Lane drew the same conclusions to his instantaneous debate that I had mine. *Screw it! The guy has cancer! These are stressful times. Take a risk and go for it!* In three-quarters of a second, Lane blurted out, "OK, honey, let's go down to the car and get the rubber gloves." We erupted in laughter! Unanticipated and unbridled laughter entered the room and

35

kicked fear's scrawny ass. We bitch-slapped stress and illness and depression. It was the first skirmish of my war with cancer, and we had won. And with my response, "No, Lane, this time no gloves," we kicked cancer while it was down. We spat on it and made fun of it and told it that it was stupid and ugly and so was its mother.

At that moment, my close friends knew I was emotionally OK. Perhaps more importantly, Christa and I knew I was OK. Sure, we suspected there were some terrible times ahead and we were not finished crying, but I then knew that laughter would play a part in my ongoing fight.

But, laughter was NOT going to be a part of the next huge task ahead; informing our three sons and our daughter-in-law that the pathologists had found cancer cells in my biopsies. You can get away with that with friends; you can't get away with it with your kids. Since they all lived out of town, we would be relying on Alexander Graham Bell's damned invention once again, so we would not be able to give them a calming look straight in the eye. We still had a huge task ahead of us. *Damn you again, Bell.*

Christa and I agreed that we should wait until we had visited Dr. Polito's office and had gathered some important facts and answers to our questions before we laid this news on the doorsteps of our children. Greg took his time as he educated us on the basics of prostate cancer. He reminded us that most prostate cancers are normally very slow growing, so we had some time to decide what we wanted to do. Greg told us about the very latest treatment options that included tremendous advancements in radiation therapies. He told us that prostate cancers were not uncommon, that most elderly men when they die have some cancerous cells in their prostate glands. He was a comforting voice during a terrifying time. Finally, he recommended that a man my age, 52 years old and in otherwise good health, have his prostate surgically removed. He talked about the new "nerve sparing" surgical procedures that had been developed, which reduce the risks of incontinence and impotence. "Incontinence and impotence"... they sound like partners in a bad law firm. They're bad partners, alright. They are the miserable duo that just about every man who is considering surgery or radiation on his prostate will be forced to confront.

We spent much of that Friday afternoon outlining, and then rehearsing the way we would present this to our kids. We had raised three sons; I was always proud of that fact. Not because boys are special, but because having three boys just seemed so unique, so rare. The night late in March of 1983 that Stephen, my youngest son was born, I called my good friend Lee Perry at 3 in the morning and excitedly delivered the news with the TV trivia question, "Lee, can you name this tune?", and then began humming the theme music to the old Fred MacMurray sitcom *My Three Sons*. I thought it was an extremely clever way of announcing that I had a third son in my family. It was Lee's wife Carol I'd rattled awake at that outrageous hour and who handed the phone to him with the aggravated warning, "It's Jerry on the phone, and I think he's been drinking".

All three of our sons are intelligent, loving, sensitive young men; Daniel, born in 1978, who was newly married to Karen, a young woman he had met while attending school at Northern Arizona University and whom we love like she is our own child (it is very cool finally having a daughter in the family); Brian, born in 1981, a University of California at Santa Barbara graduate who had settled down in that beautiful community; and, Stephen, born in 1983, who was attending UCLA and planning to go to law school after graduating. All four of them had been excellent students in high school and college. All four had developed tough competitive attitudes academically and the boys had performed at the highest levels in high school sports. They were all very sensitive to the fact that I was going through a cancer threat and they regularly called or visited home to check on Christa's and my emotional well-being. And, since we hated that we were inflicting emotional pain on our children, we were constantly keeping tabs on them to make sure they were handling the stress well, too. The simple medical truth is my three young sons were now at risk of having inherited some nasty prostate cancer gene from their dear old dad.

We placed three separate calls that Saturday morning and told the frightening facts three times. "We don't want you to be scared, but I got my biopsy report back and the doctors found some prostate cancer cells. Dr. Polito says it's slow growing, so we have time to carefully learn about treatments." We very specifically included the positive and upbeat outlook that had been shared with us. In response, they asked great questions. "Where will you go next? Do you get a second opinion? Do you have to have surgery or is radiation available?" They were concerned about our emotional states, as well, and wanted to know how we were handling the stress. They told us they loved us and asked what they could do to help. Christa and I hung up from the final call and exhaustedly looked at one another and asked, *"Oh, my God, what do we do now?"*

* * *

Soon, I was thanking God for my family and friends. Their guidance and support, suggestions and humor helped me develop an intelligent plan of attack on my disease. One of the first of my friends to have a major influence on my actions was Jay Williams, a gentle man who had recently come to work at TLC Inc. Jay and I had struck an immediate

39

friendship when we met during his first week of employment, and I quickly learned that his wisdom and experiences seemed somehow mystically related to my own.

Jay was born in the small town of McAlester, OK, not dissimilar from my Iowa birthplace. He was the star of his high school sports teams and his desire to improve his life had brought him west. I learned early in our friendship, before I ever had an inkling of my own prostate problems, that Jay was a prostate cancer survivor who learned to love his life. He wanted to educate men about the disease that he'd found so difficult to research when it was thrust upon him in the mid-1990s. Once I started to confide in Jay and expressed concerns about my own condition, he gently doled out information to me about PSA numbers and Gleason scores, hormones, surgery and radiation. He warned me about the discomforts surrounding the biopsy procedure and actually drove me to and from the urologist's office where mine was done. When I was feeling defeated, Jay would encourage me to keep fighting and offer new words of wisdom. If I had a thousand wishes, one of them would be that every cancer patient might have a loving, educated and dedicated friend like Jay Williams in his life.

Jay's only request of me was that I "pay it forward". My prostate cancer mentor encouraged me to be a friend to the next guy who was in need. He knew that men were ignorant about their prostates and about prostate cancer and that their macho attitudes were hurting their chances of beating the disease. I took Jay's words to heart and have since educated many men with prostate problems. The writing of this book is at least partly due to the healthy attitude Jay Williams taught me then and is still teaching me today.

C.H.O.P. E.M. O.F.F.

"The friends I made in college were lifelong, and the lessons I learned were invaluable. I'll admit that I haven't had a chance to use what I learned about parliamentary procedure, and I've never again had to make a bong out of a toilet paper roll, but who knows? Someday I might."
Drew Carey

The act of creating comedy, starting with a blank page and developing an idea into something that will make people laugh, has been a major part of my adult life. Let me share with you how I first learned that I could be a comedy writer and how I honed my skills.

As a biology major at California State University at Fullerton in 1974, our small class of seniors specializing in genetics was handed a task I detested. We were told we would have to debate assigned topics in front of a contingent of freshman students. My charge was to defend the

43

philosophical position that the public had the right to permanently sterilize individuals with genetic defects to help eliminate those irregularities from the world's gene pool. That's right; I got to support the idea that we could remove genetic problems from the general population by sterilizing innocent people. *What bullshit!* I hated the assignment and I hated the proposal I was being forced to support and defend. *Couldn't I just write another meaningless paper? Couldn't I "compare and contrast" something? Couldn't I paint the professor's house?* Nope, she stood firm and the date for the debate was scheduled.

Cal State Fullerton was not one of those private colleges with one professor allotted to every 14 students. This was no private school. Not even close. No, Fullerton State was a commuter campus in Orange County, CA, with about 7 million students enrolled. Most of them were just trying to stay out of the Vietnam War; 12 of them were serious about their academics. I was not among the 12. And none of the 12 were in the unwashed masses of incoming students who were required to take a freshman biology course as part of their general education units. Freshman biology was held in a giant theater-like classroom with walls of seated teenagers who were so bored that their most challenging task each day was to keep from passing out and slumping forward onto the semi-comatose kid sitting in front of them. You would be hard pressed to find an audience more undisciplined and more disinterested in issues surrounding advanced genetics than the one I was being told to address.

I had decided to major in biology years earlier for no justifiable reason, other than I was getting decent grades in science and I was hoping to see naked female bodies in anatomy class. I clearly understood the complexities of the DNA molecule and I could stain a tissue sample with the best of them. Over the subsequent years, the formal name for DNA, deoxyribonucleic acid, has come in handy dozens of times when I simply needed some biological bullshit words to top off a punch line. Make a note of that one, all you budding young comedy geniuses, take it from a guy who got his degree in biology. Also jot down and be prepared to use at a moment's notice, other biology-related terms like "epididymis", "Erlenmeyer flask" and "oozing cold sore". You're sure to get big laughs.

Back at debate-preparation headquarters in the kitchen of the small house I had rented with my wife, I envisioned myself nervously pacing before the bank of pimple-faced, hung-over 18-year-olds who deeply resented having to listen to a handful of science nerds ramble on with a bunch of jargon they did not even begin to understand or care about. The thought of publicly defending a position I did not believe in made me want to completely shut down, both mentally and emotionally; I wanted to run. I had trouble researching the issue because it was 1974 and Al Gore hadn't even begun to think about creating the Internet. I had no desire to actually read about the topic in any of the books we were forced to buy for the class, and I was essentially clueless as to the location of the college library. I knew it was somewhere on the north side of the campus because I lost a damn good Frisbee in the bushes there once; it was one of the really heavy ones that usually flew flat and straight. But I was emotionally incapable of formulating a credible position because I so vehemently opposed the viewpoint I was told I must defend.

Then it dawned on me that there was another way to address the freshman students to get their attention and come out on top in the debate while not actively supporting the compulsory neutering of millions of people. If I could not win their minds by presenting the best position on an issue none of them really cared about, I might be able to win their hearts if I could make them laugh. I sat down and began to work on presentation ideas that I thought were funny. In developing my debate strategies, I made two very important moves early on that worked in my favor. First, I stocked my refrigerator with Coors and I drank a lot of it. Next, I sought the blessing of my professor. We will call her Dr. N here to protect her identity. I told Dr. N that I was going to put together a comedy piece about the "mandated sterilization" issue and I wanted to be certain that she would allow me to present it. She was okay with the concept of the humorous presentation, but she wanted to see the details before I stood up in a state-owned classroom and potentially humiliated all of us in front of the freshman jury. After all, she had a reputation and a job to worry about; I, on the other hand, had neither.

The next decisive step I took in preparing my comedy bit was to mentally envision exactly what "sterilization" means. Hey, when you have shotgunned (a beer-drinking term that had not been invented in 1974, but that doesn't mean we weren't doing it back then) 27 beers while stretched out in a beanbag chair (the very latest high-end piece of living room furniture in the home of the completely broke college student), and you can't stop seeing in your mind's eye the image of 10 long-haired guys who had "streaked" naked across campus earlier that day in some kind of mindless, alcohol-induced protest to encourage world peace and racial harmony, suddenly the definition of sterilization was easy. It meant "removing men's testicles." It's that simple and straightforward; you just cut the guy's nuts off. The fact that I was completely ignoring any sterilization needs for the genetically marred female of the species did not seem to

47

matter to me at the time. So all I had to do was create a comedy bit about removing the "old coin purse" from every prepubescent male with a hair lip. And my presentation needed to be so funny that no one would notice it was completely lacking in substance. What was the big challenge there?

Firmly in my favor, I believed, would be shock value. Dr. N told me that in all the years she had been giving this assignment to college seniors, no one had ever tried to use comedy as part of their presentation. *What a complete surprise; no science bonehead before me had ever before tried to be funny in class.* So I had the distinct advantage of forging new ground and presenting my audience with material they did not expect to hear.

After I had canned a handful of unappealing presentation ideas, Dr. N finally approved the one I outlined for her. She allowed me to mockingly propose the establishment and funding of a governmental agency that would be assigned the absurd job of identifying and sterilizing individuals with genetic defects. The proposition would be so ridiculous that even the freshmen would see how ludicrous the concept was. Finally, it was time for the debate. Before class, I wrote the name of my proposed agency on the chalk board. In huge letters I printed:

Children's

Health and

Opportunity

Program for the

Establishment and

Maintenance of

Optimal

Familial (Gene)

Frequencies

Pretty impressive, huh? Don't try to make sense of it. It boils down to a fairly random grouping of genetics-related lingo that somehow sounds reasonably intelligent when the words are jammed together and said quickly. At the beginning of my argument, I made a brief introductory statement of the stand I was taking, shared some basic genetics information to let Dr. N know that I had at least thumbed through the textbooks, and then I turned to the chalkboard. The explanation that a huge federal bureaucracy would be a viable solution to a problem that didn't really exist

49

seemed a reasonable premise to my audience. I glanced over at Dr. N who was standing off to the side at the front of the room where she could watch the students' facial expressions and body language, and she gave just the hint of a smile. With a big arcing swipe of my eraser-filled hand at the exact moment when 500 students were saying, "What the fuck is he talking about...?," I unveiled the acronym of my newly proposed agency whose sole purpose was to sterilize innocent men. The cold, absurd name:

CHOP 'EM OFF.

"That's right ladies and gentlemen of the freshman class, I propose that an agency of the federal government be created and funded by the genetically healthy taxpayer, your mothers and fathers, to help rid our nation of the calamity of inherited defects. You've heard of NASA and NATO. Well, we'll call our new agency CHOP 'EM OFF. Sterilize everyone and anyone who might be passing on some genetic deficiency and the gene pool will become 'pure as the new driven snow'." Dr. N knowingly chuckled to herself, delighted that she'd been made privy to the joke well in advance. She watched the freshmen suddenly begin to consider what they were hearing and seeing. My debate opponent was stunned and nervously began thumbing through her prepared pages of notes. The freshman students were at first shocked and quiet, and then they roared with laughter. They suddenly sat up and paid attention. Best of all, they applauded! *What? The freshmen sat up and paid attention; they applauded?* I had taken one huge, risky swing of the humor bat and I had hammered a Mickey Mantle-sized home run over the center field fence. The fact that I had nothing of value to offer during the remainder of my presentation simply did not matter; I had already provided that elusive something of which my opponent could not even dream. I made them laugh. Yes, the freshmen voted and I won the contest, even though my debate-superior colleague had out-researched me, out-studied me, out-presented me and was much smarter than me. When the torturous hour was complete and the freshmen began to escape to the free world, I heard comments like "That was great!', "I've never seen anything like that before!" and "Does anyone know where the library is? Yeah, I do; I found a Frisbee in the bushes near there."

I knew then that there was a place for me in the world of comedy. It would be decades later that I would actually start to sharpen my skills and make some money at it.

* * *

In the mid-1990s, the *Los Angeles Times* began printing a daily joke-filled column called "Laugh Lines". In it, they would include the funniest punch lines from Jay Leno's and David Letterman's monologues of the previous evening, they

51

would showcase jokes from a few lesser-known comedy writers whom they quietly paid to help fill the new and empty space, and they invited the public to fax in original jokes. I loved this feature of the *Times*. I could not wait to fish my copy of the newspaper out of the gutter where the paperboy delivered it every morning and to pull the waterlogged pages apart so I could read the column and get everyone's humorous take on the day's world events. (I am rather sentimentally using the term "paperboy" here like there was some fourth grader breathlessly pedaling by the house at dawn every morning and innocently attempting to fling folded newspapers onto subscribers' front porches. However, these were not the old days, when the next-door neighbor's kid would shyly knock on the front door to collect subscription money once a month and be docked for every newspaper that was not paid for. No, my "paperboy" was a 45-year-old parolee driving a beat-up pickup truck with no license plates at 4 in the morning who hadn't made it home yet after drinking all night with his buddies.) The column consistently contained topical humor that would make me laugh out loud.

It took me more than a year to work up the nerve to send them my first ingenious creation. Joke writing is an emotionally risky business. We're not talking about jotting down a few ideas on a small slip of paper that you tuck away so you can read it later. No, this was the blending of a string of words that you anticipate will make strangers laugh. It takes some nerve to craft a homemade joke and cast it out into the world for everyone to scrutinize, evaluate and criticize. I finally decided to take the risk. The story in the newspaper that caught my eye that day said one of our space agencies had launched a satellite to help "map the solar system". I faxed a simple one line set-up for the joke followed by the punch line, "it will take them several days just to re-fold the map". The next morning, the entire bit, accredited to me, was printed in the *Los Angeles Times*, and the adrenaline rushed through me. My joke had been accepted by the *Times*, and it was right there with Jay Leno's material. What a thrill! I began submitting numerous jokes each day. Nearly every time I sent in a joke, the *Los Angeles Times* would print it.

After just a couple of weeks, the editor of the column, a nice guy and veteran newspaper man named Charlie Waters, began accrediting my jokes to "Comedy Writer Jerry Perisho". I quickly called the newspaper to track down Charlie so I could introduce myself and straighten him out, saying I was just a guy running a local business, not a comedy writer. His momentous words to me that morning, words that still ring loudly in my ears to this day, were, "Oh no, we read your stuff every day, Jerry. You are definitely a comedy writer!" An unbiased third party, a man who was reviewing hundreds, if not thousands of high-quality jokes every day for the *L.A. Times*, a man of obviously great intellect and virtue, voluntarily said he thought I was funny. And I was hooked. I became a regular contributor to the column and my jokes appeared there several times per week for years.

It was a wonderful way to be introduced to the world of comedy writing. Angry weapons-carrying postal workers were inspiration for hundreds of jokes. The three-ring circus known as the O.J. Simpson murder trial taking place not far from my home at the Los Angeles County Criminal Courts Building set our judicial system on its ear and was so sadly inefficient it was hilarious. And our testosterone-driven President Bill Clinton assisted White House intern Monica Lewinsky into the Oval Office and under his desk, and comedy writers rejoiced. We lived in a joke-rich environment and I loved having my material mixed in every morning with the likes of Leno and Letterman and Conan O'Brien and Dennis Miller. Soon I was also sending my sports material directly to Tom FitzGerald, a terrific veteran sportswriter for the *San Francisco Chronicle* whose syndicated column appeared in newspapers across the country. Literally thousands of my jokes were printed in the *L.A. Times* and the *San Francisco Chronicle* and the *Seattle Times* and in hundreds of newspapers and periodicals across the country. They have been printed in *Reader's Digest* and in hilarious books like *You Don't Say* by Hartley Miller.

While it became easy to get my material printed in the paper, the *L.A. Times* was not paying me for my work. Getting someone to pay you for your material is a much bigger challenge and a completely different game. There is a small market for freelance comedy writers. Comedians are looking for new jokes and ideas and concepts, and morning drive-time radio disc jockeys are desperate for comedy material when they stumble into work bleary-eyed and often hung over at 3:30 in the morning. So even though it was fun to occasionally hear Leno or Letterman recite a joke I'd written, to hear their audience laugh and to receive the pittance that they would pay a freelancer for his hard work, there was actual money to be made in writing comedy for radio. My friend Alan Ray at a company called TeleJoke, one of the original names in the *L.A. Times* column and a veteran joke writer, helped me map out a business strategy that would be successful and in 1996 I established and began marketing my comedy writing business to radio station program managers and disc jockeys around the country.

With the help of United Stations Radio Network in New York, I began to distribute my material to dozens of radio clients. From the largest radio markets of Los Angeles, New York and Chicago to the smallest like Spearfish, SD, and Nampa, ID, dozens of radio stations used my material and their checks never once bounced. I loved writing monologue material every evening, which each of these vastly diverse radio markets would find entertaining. My joke writing improved and my reputation as a quality writer became established.

For nearly 10 years I worked as a corporate executive during the day and a professional freelance comedy writer at night. For about four hours each night, Sunday through Thursday, I researched the day's news and created two pages of monologue material (about 20 jokes per night) for my growing list of clients. I had a thriving business until the day in 2004 that I learned I had prostate cancer. That evening I sat down and emailed my clients. I explained my new situation and closed down my joke writing enterprise. I could not be funny at night; I knew I would be too tired from fighting the daily emotional, and finally physical, battle with cancer.

Crushing Walnuts, Loving the RoboSapien and Hating The Company With No Soul

"It's true that misery loves company. If you ever doubt that, look at a No-Pest Strip. It's covered with flies. You'd think that the first fly would tell any others, 'Go around! Go around!'"
Margaret Smith

K nowing that I had cancer growing inside my body and that every day that passed may result in it being more difficult to treat the disease made the next few weeks one of the most difficult periods my wife and I faced. When I was diagnosed in mid-September of 2004, Dr. Polito had warned that Christa and I should plan to take action before the end of the year. And if you really think about it, who wouldn't want to top off their Christmas celebrations with a painful New Year's recovery from prostate surgery? *Maybe we could schedule it for New Year's Eve, and they could install a catheter that whistles and shoots confetti every time I take a leak.* On one hand, we were incredibly fortunate that a variety of options were available to us. On the other hand, every treatment option brought along with it a wagon load of undesirable side effects.

In fact, there was a whole smorgasbord of treatment options. All of them offered excellent cure rates as long as your cancer was confined to your prostate gland, and all of them carried terrible side effects. To carry out the smorgasbord analogy, it's like having a wide array of foods to choose from, but when you're done eating any of the entrees, they're all going to make you puke on yourself. Surgery, whether via the traditional removal of the prostate with a long pubic incision or the new robot-assisted laparoscopic type, presented the very possible end-result of not being able to control my urine flow and never again being able to get a boner. So, in the part of my mind that produces worst-case scenarios, assuming I lived through the operation, surgery presented a potentially intercourse-free future where I'd be walking around with a rivulet of pinkish-yellow pee running down my leg and trailing behind me wherever I went. Radiation therapy, whether with an external beam or with the implantation of tiny radioactive seeds directly into the prostate (called brachytherapy), offered good results, but it would leave the diseased prostate inside my body, and I am not happy about that; I want it out. Otherwise, it would be

y

58

like having the xenomorph from the *Alien* movies crawling around inside of me. I'd keep waiting for its head to burst through my skin and eat somebody. With cryotherapy, doctors can freeze the cells of the prostate and theoretically kill the cancer cells. Basically, you turn your prostate gland into a gelato with the risk of standing at the urinal and pissing mini ice cubes.

Adding significant stress to our lives beyond the treatment dilemmas was the fact that TLC Inc. had been sold to The Company With No Soul and the transition to the new regime was beginning. The CEO of The Company With No Soul, in an address to the entire employee base of TLC, had repeatedly promised that "nothing is going to change; we're going to keep things just the way they are." Please notice the quotation marks around those words. That is exactly what the man said. Verbatim. In other words, everything was about to change.

Mr. Crica (Crica is not his real last name), the regional vice president of The Company With No Soul and the man who was to become my immediate boss, was a raging egomaniac who would repeatedly look you in the eye and call you by the wrong name. Whenever he entered a room and bellowed "How are you today?" he insisted everyone cheerily shout back to him in unison, "Great!" Like robots, we were to tell him we felt great, whether you had a sick child at home, were going through a divorce or had prostate cancer. We were supposed to convince him that, no matter what was happening in our simple lives, we felt great working for The Company With No Soul, and especially working for him. Everyone quickly learned how absolutely ineffective this guy was. At TLC, we had been used to dealing with the actual problems an employer encounters, and we strived to provide good customer service in a very competitive industry and market while making TLC a pleasant place to establish a career. Now we were to be throttled with the narrow-minded machinations of an ego freak. We discovered that, rather than create an environment that fostered employee satisfaction, Crica mandated that everyone tell him they were feeling "great" in an apparent effort to make them all believe it. It was most certainly a failed attempt to make him appear to be a management genius.

I didn't feel great, and I refused to be a part of this little "Stepford slaves" ritual. I never responded to his room-entry theatrics by shouting that I was great. Had he ever confronted me about my silence, I was prepared to get directly in his grill and bark, "I am not great. I have cancer and quite frankly I am having trouble marshalling the energy to drag my butt into the office to work for you every day." It was well rehearsed in my head, but some interloper had clued Crica in to the fact that I was laying for him.

Trying to figure out what Crica and company expected of me, I scheduled a meeting with him in his office where he made me wait the 25 minutes designed to show me just exactly who was in charge. Finally sitting across the desk from him, I asked him to describe his work style and to give me a sense of what he wanted to see from me in the upcoming 12 months. At the time, meeting with my new supervisor seemed a very reasonable thing to do. I got a mind-numbing 90-minute sermon about the way they used to do things at the even bigger who-gives-a-damn-about-the-little-guy mega-corporation where he'd previously been employed. He never touched on a single operating issue pertaining to The Company With No Soul. I never got one tangible answer to my long list of questions. His primary message to me that afternoon was, "Remember Jerry, it is far easier to beg for forgiveness than it is to ask for permission." At least he got my name right. But he was instructing me to do anything, even if it was outside company policy, to get a task done and then to beg him to forgive me for breaking the rules. The man had no leadership skills. I didn't know this guy, and I certainly didn't trust that he had my best interests at heart. He was setting me up, and setting up anyone else who bothered to sit with him the way I did, to be terminated. What a terrible management style!

Christa and my sons encouraged me to leave The Company With No Soul. They reminded me that life is short and my health was too important to waste on people I did not respect. I made the decision that I could not stay, but the realities that I would be without the firm's health insurance coverage and that I would not be drawing an income made the decisions surrounding treatment of the cancer all the more difficult.

Sadly, when you get the news you have cancer, there are no decision-making charts or user-friendly computer programs to assist you. There is no medical playbook that helps you intelligently and confidently orchestrate your sequence of moves. This is a very serious weakness in the world of medicine. While I applaud doctors and hospitals and researchers in general for their advancements in diagnosing and treating disease, they have forgotten to create a system that tenderly guides the sick patient through the maze with which only the medical professionals and health insurance policy administrators are so familiar. Too many suffering human beings are left weaponless to fend for themselves in a brand new wilderness that is rife with fire-breathing medical dragons, diagnostic demons and bureaucratic beasts.

I was lucky. I had a wife who took good notes and helped me ask good questions whenever we visited a new doctor. Dr. Polito had recommended surgery at our local hospital, but logic and a fairly broad base of medical knowledge told me to get a second opinion. (Don't forget, I graduated from Cal State Fullerton 30 years earlier with a biology degree, so I could pretty much get into any medical school I wanted.) And networking with a wide range of friends kept me moving in the right direction.

One afternoon, I took up the offer for assistance made by my buddy Lane Thomas. A friend of Lane's had been diagnosed with prostate cancer and had completed robotically assisted laparoscopic surgery at City of Hope National Medical Center just a few months earlier. I spoke with Lane's friend, and he recommended that I see Dr. Tim Wilson, the head of urology there. He was so pleased with the outcome of his surgery and felt he was having so few side effects that he didn't hesitate to make the recommendation to me. He used terms like, "I almost never need to use a pad when I go out for brief periods of time," and "It's been a couple of months and I am working pretty much full time now." It was a clear reminder to me that this surgery, even in a best-case scenario, could be devastating.

So, I planned to go to City of Hope to see if I was a likely candidate for the robotic surgery and to see what the doctor might recommend. But, when the hospital called my HMO for approval of the visit, my insurer told them I was not covered; they were not in my plan. *What?!* They refused to pay for a simple office visit, let alone an operation that utilized the most modern technology, but was not within their restrictive blueprint. They were treating the latest most high-tech method of prostate surgery like it was some kind of Rube Goldberg contraption created by an eighth grade science class. The seemingly simple desire to obtain a second opinion for treatment of prostate cancer from an extremely well respected medical provider, a hospital specializing in cancer treatments that was located just 20 minutes from my home, suddenly became a potential impossibility. It felt like the HMO was giving me their version of a prostate exam themselves, telling me to stick my second opinion where the sun has never shined. I had already had enough of those experiences, and I was not going to accept this from them without a fight.

I took a day of vacation from work at The Company With No Soul and dedicated it to getting The Insurer With No Heart to approve my request. At 9 a.m. sharp, I sat down with the telephone and my list of phone numbers, and I promised myself I would get this appointment for a second opinion approved by the insurance company and scheduled at the hospital. I had cancer, and my life was at risk. No New York insurance salesman with the personality of a door stop

64

was going to keep me from visiting the doctor or the hospital I wanted to see.

That day, in the span of five hours, I made eight phone calls to my family practice doctor, encouraging him to apply pressure on my behalf with The Insurer With No Heart; after all it was his medical group that was a part of the HMO plan, which was giving me all this grief. I made seven calls to City of Hope National Medical Center to encourage employees in various positions there to make the appointment without the approval of the insurer; they wouldn't. And I placed 17 calls to different people at The Insurer With No Heart. If I didn't get an answer I liked from one unsympathetic employee, I asked to speak to that person's supervisor. If someone promised to call me back at a specific time, but didn't, I called them and asked why I hadn't heard from them. "I've got cancer," I would remind them. "This is life and death to me." And I truly felt that it was. "I have to get this done today," I would tell them, "I am taking a day off work for this." *Thank you, Alexander Graham Bell, for your wonderful telephonic creation. And say hello to your able assistant Watson.* Never once did I set the telephone down in that five hour period and Verizon's stock rose sharply.

With every person I spoke to that day, I was courteous and businesslike, and I didn't let them know I thought their company sucked. Though I occasionally shouted an obscenity after hanging up in frustration, I never swore at anyone with whom I spoke. Finally, I simply wore down the paper-pushers working for The Insurer With No Heart. A supervisor, a wonderful, warm woman whose name I have in my notes but whose identity I promised to protect, agreed to *not* follow company protocol. She hand-typed a letter of approval on company letterhead and faxed it to City of Hope. Victory for the little guy. The hospital called me and we set a date for my appointment with Dr. Wilson.

I sat and cried that afternoon. Mostly, I cried because I was so happy that an appointment with a top medical center had been made. But I also cried because I had learned firsthand that my health insurance company was not looking out for my health. Instead, they were trying to minimize the financial impact on their bottom line. If they could wiggle out of paying for the visit to the doctor, and ultimately for the cost of the proposed high-tech surgery, they would save themselves a big medical payment. The only reason I got my way that day was because my persistence started costing them money in employee time. They had expected me to roll over and comply with their decision and I was one of the few who fought them. It was hand-to-hand combat, and I had won a battle in what was shaping up to be a long, uncomfortable war.

For a patient, an introductory visit to a cancer hospital is a frightening and terribly disorienting event. It is a tangible admission to a fact that you don't really want to face. You are seriously ill; you have cancer. Don't get me wrong, the people at City of Hope were wonderful. In fact, when we received the mailed confirmation of our consultation appointment, they thoughtfully invited us to use their valet parking services free of charge, a courtesy to the newbie patient. When we pulled up to the half-moon driveway outside the hospital's entrance, the attendant on duty opened my car door and warmly said, "Welcome to City of Hope; we're glad you're here." I paused as I swung one leg out of my car because I found that greeting courteous and at the same time oddly disquieting. While I was pleased that his tone of voice was reassuring, almost calming, I subconsciously asked myself why this man, whom I had never met before this very moment, would be glad that I had cancer. "Why would he be glad that I had to come here?" I wondered. Of course, upon further reflection, what else could he say, "Welcome to City of Hope; sorry you've got the 'Big C'?" Or maybe he could have comforted me with, "Park your own damn car Cancer Boy. Can't you see I'm on a break?" I had to remind myself that I was the one in the heightened state of sensitivity and that the man who greeted me in a very kind tone was simply doing his job. In fact, he was doing it well.

City of Hope is a 217-bed Comprehensive Cancer Center located on 112 acres in eastern Los Angeles County. It is a busy, bustling place with people laughing in one portion of the lobby while a bathrobed patient wearing a bandana to cover her bald head and who is hooked up to a half-dozen bottles of potent chemotherapy drugs shuffles by to get a bit of exercise and fresh air. Everybody we met that day treated us with respect. They treated us like we were members of a loving family. They seemed to intuitively know that Christa and I were scared so bad our knees were literally shaking. They reassured us that we'd be okay, and they walked us through the maze of corridors and hallways to offices and departments we'd never before visited. We waited nervously to meet Dr. Wilson.

Finally, we were called into an examination room and were asked to wait for a moment. Dr. Wilson arrived. You know how you meet certain people in your life who are so smart and so energetic that you can look in their eyes and see the wheels turning in their minds? There is a sparkle in their eyes. It's like, regardless of how fast you are running on your own cognitive treadmill, they are always at least a couple of steps ahead. Oh, they stay close enough to chat with you when they want, but you know they could accelerate to Mach

III at a moment's notice. Well, that's what we saw in Dr. Tim Wilson when he entered the examination room that afternoon. He was smart, had a good sense of humor, he was perceptive and he had practiced the robotic surgical procedure on more than 500 men in preparation for working on me. He offered direct and informed answers to every question we fired at him. He assured us that the robot offered innumerable advantages over the old-fashioned traditional surgery and that at my relatively young age (I was 52, and prostatectomy is an old man's surgery) I would tolerate the operation well. In fact, he said there would be so little loss of blood that I would not need to accumulate and store units of my own blood prior to surgery. He talked about how he can see the entire surgical field inside the patient's body, thanks to the laparoscopic lights and cameras that are used. He explained that much of the internal suturing done during the traditional prostatectomy operation is done blindly, strictly by the surgeon's sense of touch. (In a later visit with a surgeon who utilizes the traditional surgical techniques, that doctor stressed the advantages of being able to touch the surgical field, an advantage that the robotic method did not provide. This information did nothing but "muddy the waters" and make our decision more difficult. It also illustrated that professionals in each discipline would speak most highly about their own area of expertise.)

Over the span of several weeks, we spoke with brilliant people. Radiologists told us how their method of attacking the problem was the least invasive, whether we chose to have a series of radiation beam treatments or if we elected to go with radioactive seeds being implanted in the gland. Oncologists explained that amazing strides were being made in the chemical treatment of prostate cancer. While advances that would be present within just a few years were not going to help me and my current problem, we learned that prostate cancer would be less of a problem, less of a threat to my three sons, all of whom were now at a higher risk of developing the disease. Christa and I both knew that Dr. Wilson and the people at City of Hope had made the most positive impression on us. We agreed that radiation was not a reasonable choice for us because we both wanted the cancerous gland out of my body. I decided that I was going to put my life in the capable and experienced hands of Dr. Tim Wilson.

The next time I sat at my dining room table and cried was the day I got my surgery scheduled at City of Hope with Dr. Wilson. Something magical happens when the decisions have been made and the plans are firmly in place to fight your cancer. A wave of pride and accomplishment washed over me. This time I cried with sheer relief because I felt I was on my way to being cured.

My family and close friends proved to be invaluable sources of strength to Christa and me. Regular calls from sons Steve, Dan and Brian always included the sarcastically obligatory question, "Oh yeah, and what's new with you, Cancer Boy?" As a family, we continued to not allow cancer to dominate our lives. We refused to allow cancer to take the fun out of our conversations.

Although Christa and I found ourselves emotionally spent at each day's end, we tried to maintain our normal social activities, which included dinner with friends on Friday nights. The Thomases, along with Faye and Frank Hill, who were longtime friends and whose kids grew up with ours, and Vicki Lopez, Christa's sister whom I had known since we all were in junior high school together, would find a nice restaurant to commandeer for a couple of hours and we would decompress. Quite frankly, it never dawned on me to be anything but open and honest with this wonderful group of friends when I learned that I had cancer. I had no reason to be embarrassed, and I needed their love and support. I knew they would help me deal with this scary new challenge.

Prostate cancer became a standard punch line for this group. As people began to pile into one of our SUV's heading out to eat, someone would sarcastically shout, "Oh, does Cancer Boy need to ride shotgun again? Let him have

71

his way. Don't worry about it, Jerry. We'll be fine cramped here in the back. Man, I will be glad when this surgery is done and this bunch of malarkey is behind us." Black humor was alive and well with this group.

After my Dec. 1 surgery was scheduled and as Thanksgiving approached, my friends started asking me more serious details about how the operation would work. They wanted to know about the robotics involved in the high-tech procedure and what the aftereffects of the surgery would include. The details of the robotics were amazing and fun to discuss, but the anticipated aftereffects of the surgery were quite depressing. Each of them was astounded that a surgeon could complete this operation by merely controlling the robotic arms and tools while peering into a monitor offering a three-dimensional view of my insides. I told them that once my catheter was removed about a week after the operation, I would be wearing some kind of pad just in case I had trouble controlling my urine flow. I explained that this was common with men having this type of surgery. One night at dinner, in a strong showing of team unity, my good friend Frank Hill put his hand across to the middle of the table and loudly invited everyone, "Let's take a pledge." Everyone's hands went in. "As long as Jerry wears a pad, we all wear a pad." "Yeah," our group cheered agreement. Next, I quickly reached my hand to the middle of the table, which attracted the others, and added, "If that's the case, let's go all out. As long as Jerry wears a catheter, we all wear a catheter." We sealed the pledges with a toast. It was a week or so later that I presented each of the "pledgers" their own personalized adult diapers, their names imperfectly scribbled across the crotch with black marker, and individualized catheters and urine bags, constructed from two feet of clear thick plastic tube masking taped into a white kitchen trash bag. A week later, I received from my friends a RoboSapien, a remote controlled robot that would dance to music and grunt like a

The RoboSapien that made me laugh.

73

human being. He walked into our home carrying a walnut in his right claw, symbolizing the walnut-sized prostate that was soon to be yanked out by a robot.

At another evening dinner with this group of troublemakers, Christa began describing the difficulty we were having finding a new bedroom set, one which would include a couple of dressers, some night stands and a new king bed, replacing the queen bed we'd had since our wedding. With perfect timing, Frank Hill suggested that Christa put off making any kind of a purchase, pointing out that, "depending on how Jerry's operation goes, you might be able to get by with a twin." Black humor, a death joke; it was a death joke that Frank knew would be OK with me and he suspected our group would appreciate, as well. When I started laughing, everyone started laughing. I loved it. But the people in the neighboring tables didn't think we were so funny. *Screw 'em, I have cancer.*

Karen, Dan, Stephen and Brian got into the act, too. Brian and Steve devised a ridiculous-looking trophy that featured a hand-created walnut at the top, which they proudly presented to me. On one trip to Whittier from his home in Phoenix, Dan presented me with a t-shirt emblazoned with a stylized diagram of the male urinary tract on the front. Highlighted in the middle of the illustration was the walnut-sized prostate gland. The words "Crushing Walnuts" were printed across the bottom of the illustration. "Crushing Walnuts" became a battle cry. By crushing this walnut, we were crushing cancer.

CRUSHING WALNUTS

**The Perisho family wore t-shirts with the "Crushing Walnuts"
battle cry emblazoned across the front.**

While I was willing to have a few laughs with friends and family, I fully realized that my condition was serious and the operation I was about to undergo brought with it certain very real risks. I was worried about the future of my family. What would happen to them if I died on the operating table? What would happen if they found that cancer had spread throughout my body and that it was simply not operable? Would everyone be okay? Would Christa have enough

money to survive? Had I prepared properly for the worst?
Reminders of the important things we must do in our lives
come from some of the most unusual places.

The fact that I needed to properly prepare for the
possibility of dying was driven home for me one night as I
was watching *Band of Brothers*, the great HBO series about a
unit fighting in Europe during World War II. In the scene
that so deeply hit me, Easy Company of the 101st Airborne is
packing up and preparing for the famous D-day invasion of
France. They are checking their weapons and gear, talking
amongst themselves and smoking, when one of the officers
shouts, "All right. Listen up! Listen up! If you did not sign
your GI life insurance policy, you go over and see Sergeant
Evans at the Headquarters Company tent. You boys don't let
your families miss out on $10,000."

It was a stark reminder that each of them might die.
It reminded me that I had details I needed to tend to because
I might die. Christa and I had not updated our wills for
decades. We owned a home with a lot of equity and I needed
to protect and preserve our assets, whether I was on the
operating table or not. We made a visit to the law office of
Lane Thomas, signed the notarized paperwork that he had
prepared for us, and one set of worries was taken care of.
But, the apparent finality of the moment, the realization of
what prompted the visit to my attorney, presented a strange

dichotomy. On one hand, it seemed so gloomy and desperate and sad. We were facing the fact that we were mortal, that I might die very soon. It was a frightening reality that I believe each of us resists confronting. On the other hand, having my financial matters in order provided a great sense of comfort and peace. I would not need to fear that Christa or, if Christa and I were to die together, our sons would not know where to find the documents describing what we owned and where everything was located.

A week before the surgery, the hospital wanted me to come in for a series of tests to make certain I was physically and metabolically ready for the operation. A rather curious and humorous moment occurred during this visit to the hospital. I'd had a lot of blood drawn in the prior few weeks, but this time the phlebotomist also wanted a urine sample from me. She handed me a small cup and directed me to the restroom. She also handed me a sealed moist towelette packet and clearly instructed me to "use this first". Now, I am an educated man, but I didn't know exactly what she wanted me to do with the damn thing. She knew there was soap and water in the bathroom if I needed to wash my hands, so that wasn't it. The cup looked clean as I removed it from its sealed plastic wrapping, so I didn't worry about it. I couldn't imagine they wanted me to scrub down the bathroom with a towelette; I mean, I was willing to tidy the place up a bit, but this seemed a little much. So the only conclusion I could reach was that dirty penis tips were a growing problem in the world of pathology labs. I scrubbed mine thoroughly and I am proud to report my urine sample was immaculate.

My next stop that morning was at the Radiology Department for a bone scan. Two and a half hours earlier, I'd received a painless injection of a radioactive tracer substance that had now been distributed into my bone marrow. As I stretched out on the platform near the x-ray equipment, the technician on duty, Robert, asked, "You're not claustrophobic, are you?" Then, he secured my arms and hands at my sides with Velcro straps so I could not move during the procedure. The moment I was straightjacketed into place, I became a Pavlovian experiment. We chatted about his job. When Robert said that some people's noses itch during the tests, mine did. When he said some people start to yawn, I did. It was crazy; if he'd decided to ring a bell, I would have started salivating. When the machine was moved to within 1 millimeter of my nose, I closed my eyes and figured the guy was going to have his way with me. Hey, with the number of people who'd already had their hands up my rear end, what could this guy do that was new? Thirty minutes later the procedure was completed.

I am guilty of always trying to get technicians and other hospital workers to give me some clue as to their medical opinions, so I don't have to wait some ungodly amount of time for a doctor to share the findings. I will try to befriend them and I'll look over their shoulders and ask questions like I'm a student. All I really want to know is what they've found. This day, Robert told me that in his opinion my baseline bone scan showed no "hot spots". Hot spots are locations that "light up"; they are places that have absorbed an increased amount of the radioactive tracer material and appear as bright places on the skeletal form. This could indicate a tumor, an infection, a fracture or a place where Jerry's prostate cancer had taken up residence. My nuclear scanning test results were a skeletal picture of a 6-foot, 6-inch guy with incredibly good looks and world-class wit. At least, that's what I saw.

There was in fact no cancer in my bones. That meant one thing: Look out prostatectomy, here I come!

A guy is 70 years old and loves to fish. He was sitting in his boat the other day when he heard a voice say, "Pick me up."

He looked around and couldn't see anyone. He thought he was dreaming when he heard the voice say again, "Pick me up." He looked in the water and there, floating on the top, was a frog.

The man said, "Are you talking to me?"

The frog said, "Yes, I'm talking to you. Pick me up. Then kiss me and I'll turn into the most beautiful woman you have ever seen. I'll make sure that all your friends are envious and jealous because you will have me as your bride."

The man looked at the frog for a short time, reached over, picked it up carefully, and placed it in his front breast pocket.

Then the frog said, "What, are you nuts? Didn't you hear what I said? I said kiss me and I will be your beautiful bride."

He opened his pocket, looked at the frog and said, "Nah, at my age I'd rather have a talking frog."

Author Unknown

"You, Kid With the Bad Prostate, Out of the Gene Pool"

I t is vitally important that every cancer patient know some family medical history that he is prepared to share with physicians. Here is a bit of mine and how it has affected my life.

Posed quietly amidst the rolling corn fields and criss-crossing country roads of southeastern Iowa is the sleepy community of Oskaloosa. Chief Mahaska of the Iowa tribe ruled the area around Oskaloosa a few decades before the Civil War. The land is fertile because the nearby muddy Des Moines River would overflow its banks every spring when the winter snows melted and the rain came down in buckets.

That was before the Army Corps of Engineers built the Red Rock Dam upriver in the 1960s. It is a quiet, serene setting. Local historians claim there is absolutely no truth to the oft-repeated folklore that "Oskaloosa" is an old Native American term for "do yourself a big favor and go west; this land is best viewed in the rear-view mirror of your moving van." There is not a traffic jam near the place. The chirping birds, the wind blowing through the trees, the serenity and the slow pace will either drive you batty or help to keep you emotionally grounded, depending upon the speed of your lifestyle.

Near the picturesque Oskaloosa town square, but still very close to where Highway 163 heads northwest to the state capital of Des Moines, Oliver Paul Thayer moved his Chevrolet car dealership from Eddyville in the early 1930s. What a tough time to be in business, any business. Banks were failing, manufacturing plants were closing, and people were begging for work. Mr. Thayer struggled to keep his business alive during the Depression, but he always sold enough cars to make payroll. His reputation was impeccable as a crusty home-grown businessman and boss. Everyone in southeastern Iowa loved the man they knew as "Toby". He was hard working, honest and very smart. Yeah, yeah, yeah, I know all the jokes about the rarity of honest, hard working car salesmen. I have written those punch lines a hundred times myself. If he were alive today, Toby would laugh at the jokes, create a few of his own, and tell you how appalled he is with the corruption and dishonesty of the modern business world. Then, he would tell you about the factory-installed features on the latest Chevy models and sell you a car.

Born in 1897, Toby grew up in southern Iowa. He lived his teenage years there and finally joined his father in business operating the N.A. Thayer and Son Auto and Horse Livery in nearby Eddyville. He took a few years away from work because, as he used to tell his grandkids, "I had a rich uncle who sent me to France during World War I." When asked what he did during the war, he humbly answered, "I just rode around Paris on a motorcycle." I never learned what his actual duty was, I suspect because Toby was one of those men who was not comfortable talking about their war experiences… at least not to his grandson. He returned from the war to end all wars to focus on work and on his pursuit of young Wanda Waneta Myers.

The love of Toby's life, Wanda, also born in 1897, learned from her mother how to sew, how to garden and how to cook. Wow, could she cook! During the years that I knew her, the noon meal was always the big one during the summer months, and she would spend all morning in the kitchen orchestrating a banquet of homemade gravy noodles and mashed potatoes, gigantic ears of sweet corn on the cob covered with butter and salt, and fresh green beans accented

83

with chunks of real bacon. When the tomatoes were in season, they would be spread across a huge platter in the middle of the table, sliced so thick you would need your knife to cut them. She'd finish it all off with a fresh homemade rhubarb pie with a huge scoop of hand-cranked vanilla ice cream on top.

Toby won Wanda's heart, and in 1919 they were married. Wanda and Toby started growing their family quickly. Just a year after their wedding, their son William was born. A year after Grandma Thayer gave birth to my Uncle Bill, Toby and Wanda's daughter Jacqueline, my mom, arrived. Undoubtedly Toby celebrated each addition to his family the way he started the beginning of every new day, by smiling broadly, laughing robustly and by lighting up an unfiltered Lucky Strike cigarette. Luckys became a part of Toby's persona. When he was wrapping up a business deal or just talking with a friend, he would fire up a Lucky. Toby enjoyed many of the happiest events in his life by lighting up a Lucky Strike cigarette. He grieved that way, too. I'm guessing he lit one and wept years later when his sister Zoe died of ovarian cancer.

My mother, Jacqueline Yvonne Thayer, born to Wanda and Toby in 1921, was a beautiful and very athletic girl. Her infectious smile, her great sense of humor and the old-fashioned work ethic she had learned from her parents made her a strong competitor, and usually a winner, in everything she tackled. She was an excellent student and as one of the stars on the high school basketball team she rarely missed a standing set shot from 20 feet. Jackie went to local William Penn College and received her teaching credential to become an elementary school teacher. Her good looks attracted the handsome World War II B-25 bomber pilot, Lester Beryl Perisho. Jackie and Les were married in 1944 in Oskaloosa. Four years later, the first of their sons, Joel, was born, and four years after that, in 1952, I brought an unbelievable amount of joy to their lives, as you'd fully expect; the only baby ever born that never cried, never crapped in its pants and immediately went out and found a job. Of the two brothers, I was then, and remain today, the smarter and better looking. (Joel can counter that claim when he writes his own book.)

There were booming economic times following World War II and the Korean War. America thrived. Opportunity abounded. In the mid-1950s, knowing that he could succeed on his own, Les left his job at his father-in-law's Thayer Chevrolet dealership in Oskaloosa and went to work for the Allis-Chalmers Manufacturing Company, a manufacturer of heavy farm machinery headquartered in Milwaukee, WI. He was a successful salesman who advanced rapidly through the ranks of the company. But, he quickly learned that if you wanted to capitalize on any chances for promotion, you had to be willing to move to different parts of the country, places where new job openings existed. Les and Jackie moved their family from the bright lights of Oskaloosa, Iowa to the glitter and glamour of Le Sueur, MN, to the hustle and bustle of Huron, SD, and finally to the megalopolis known as Moraga, CA, in the span of just eight years. Their heads spinning from their whirlwind tour of the country, Les and Jackie asked themselves, "Where else could they send us?" The final uprooting was to the smog capital of the world, sunny Southern California. In 1960, the family settled in the community of Whittier.

In the early 1960s, my parents bought our first stereophonic record player. What a mechanical marvel it was! The sound coming out of the left speaker was slightly different from the sound coming out of the right speaker. *Wow, treble and bass settings!* For hours, I sat and listened to Bill Cosby and the Smothers Brothers comedy albums spinning on the turntable. I knew all of the cuts from their albums by heart. I listened for the impeccable timing that great comedians develop during their careers, and I was taken by their abilities to tell hilarious stories about common occurrences in their lives. The comedy was simple, clean and incredibly successful. I listened and I absorbed it through osmosis.

Basketball was a primary theme in our household. The hoop and backboard that had been bolted to the roof of our garage were like magnets that drew our family and every kid in the neighborhood to our back yard. I'm sure the pounding of the ball against the cement driveway at 1 a.m. violated at least 50 different noise ordinances on the city's books. That didn't matter. A game could start up at any moment, and anyone could get challenged.

My mom was a terrific basketball player and even in her 40s and 50s she could shoot and hit 15-foot set shots with regularity. She loved to play the game and she loved to watch her sons play. I hurt my mom very deeply the night before the first game of the season during my senior year in high school; the year was 1969. I told her that I did not want her to come and watch me play the next day. It was not that I was embarrassed at having one of my parents at a game (even I am not that big an asshole). And my reasoning was not that I was embarrassed about my own abilities; I was one of the best players on the team and the team captain. My problem was that I was afraid I would make a mistake on the court and not make her proud of me. I was afraid that however I performed that day I would fall short of her expectations, so the entire problem would be avoided if she would just stay away. What stupid, stupid reasoning. I scored 20 points that day in a losing effort and I saw the sadness in her eyes as I reported to her about the game. I quickly got over my selfish, self-centered belief that the world was somehow spinning around my skinny ass and she came to the next game, and most of those during the rest of the season. I could hear her voice in the stands, "Way to hustle, you guys!" She always told me that I'd made her proud.

Because we had moved to what many Iowans thought was a distant and foreign land, California, my family made fairly regular summer vacation trips to the Midwest to stay closely connected with my grandparents. Toby and Wanda's home was located on the main highway through Oskaloosa leading out to the cemetery on the east side of town. Back then, Iowans had a wonderful tradition of graciously pulling to the side of the highway whenever a funeral procession was in sight; it was a final demonstration of respect for the dearly departed. I saw that happen numerous times from my grandparents' front porch, a practice that simply cannot survive in today's fast-paced world. In a separate but related event, I remember as a young boy sitting with my grandfather on his front porch one afternoon when the town's funeral director walked by and waved to us. My grandpa leaned down to me and said, "Just look at him smiling at me. He's just waiting for me to 'shuffle off.'" This interaction reminds me of one of my favorite quotes from Mark Twain, "Let us so live that when we come to die even the undertaker will be sorry."

My Grandpa Thayer loved smoking cigarettes. I do not know how many packs of Lucky Strikes Toby actually consumed in his lifetime, but let's do some simple math to get an idea. Let's assume he started his nasty habit in 1920 (I suspect he began even earlier) and let's also assume he smoked one pack of 20 unfiltered cigarettes a day (in my limited personal experience, I saw him smoke more than that daily). By 1970, he would have conservatively sucked down the toxic carcinogenic tars, gases and nicotine of 365,000 cigarettes.

The recollections of summer vacations with my grandparents in Iowa are some of the best memories I own. My grandpa had a problem, though. I remember him waking up every morning during our summer visits and coughing for an hour. Every day it was the same seemingly unnatural routine, and I could not understand what was happening. Why was it that he would need to sit on the edge of his bed early each morning and hack deep, wet, horrible lung-burning coughs that never seemed to get relief? Why didn't he ever get any better? And finally, why did he light up an unfiltered Lucky Strike when he was finished coughing? I had never before seen anyone with this condition, with this addiction. I asked my mom about it, and she warned me about the

89

hazards of smoking cigarettes. I wondered to myself why this brilliant man, this hero of mine, was not heeding his daughter's advice, why he was not using simple common sense.

Toby was diagnosed with lung cancer in 1971. His doctors had warned him years earlier about smoking too much and they had urged him to cut back, but he didn't, or couldn't. He was able to negotiate the toughest car deal in town and he could catch the biggest catfish in the Des Moines River, but he was no match for the addiction of nicotine. His doctors examined him, told him it was cancer and they gave him permission to "go ahead and smoke as long as the cigarettes were filtered." *Now, there is some brilliant medical advice, huh?* My grandpa died in 1972 and left a giant painful injury on my heart. As I rode in his funeral procession, I watched as Oskaloosans pulled to the side of the highway. The hearse carrying his casket quietly passed his two-story home that was filled with countless wonderful memories. Remembering Mark Twain's famous quote, I think even Oskaloosa's undertaker was sorry to see my grandfather "shuffle off".

The following year, Wanda noticed she was passing blood in her stool when she went to the bathroom. Like so many others with similar symptoms, she was frightened at the prospect of being truly sick and she kept her condition to herself, hoping that it would just go away. Finally, after continual bleeding and several incidents of light-headedness, she went to the doctor and they confirmed she had colon cancer. Wanda Thayer, at the age of 76 years, had her cancerous colon surgically removed and was introduced to life with a colostomy bag. She did not let this new burden keep her down, though. She traveled and kept busy, and her spirits remained high. My grandma was warm and loving and wonderful; and she died in 1975. Her death left a second painful bruise on my heart. Once again, the kind people of Oskaloosa pulled to the side of the highway to say good-bye to a long-time friend.

It was that same year, 1975, that my mom, the vivacious, energetic Jackie Perisho, learned she had lymphoma, cancer of the lymph nodes and the lymphatic system. She had felt a small lump in her armpit and bravely went to the doctor without any delay. My mother had seen her parents both recently die from cancer, and she became a cancer-fighting bulldog. She decided life was too precious to give up without a battle. She scrapped and fought with a vengeance. It is her behavior that I hope I am duplicating in fighting my own battle with prostate cancer.

My mom never once hesitated to take on the available chemotherapies. And it was nasty stuff her oncologist kept giving her. They said she would lose her hair, and she did.

They said she would get sick and lose her appetite and lose weight, and she did all of those things. They said she had a good chance of getting well and she did. She beat it. She defeated lymphoma. My mom looked cancer directly in the eye and kicked its ass. But that nasty, unforgiving son-of-a-bitch did not go away completely.

Life was very good for all of us during the ensuing years. Christa and I created our own family. Joel and his wife Lois had three beautiful and brilliant children. And each of Jackie's grandchildren got to experience the joy of being hugged and kissed and loved by a grandmother who gave them all her heart. Her smile was loving, her lap was comfy and her heart was huge. My mom personified "unconditional love".

Then, in 1989, ovarian cancer reared its ugly, wicked and uncompromising head. It arrived completely un-announced to our family, with the possible exception of the death of my mother's Aunt Zoe, Toby's sister, who had died of the dreadful disease several decades earlier. We now know that ovarian cancer is one of those that travel in our DNA. Some microscopic genetic mix-up on a chromosome somewhere in her cells was causing her pain and creating havoc once again in our world.

At the time this was wracking my family, Gilda Radner's biography *It's Always Something* was in the book stores and selling well. I loved everything Gilda Radner had done over the years on *Saturday Night Live*. Her creations of Roseanne Rosannadanna and Emily Litella were incredible; they were the creations of a genius comedic mind. Gilda had been stricken with ovarian cancer, and the book chronicled her battle with the disease. I purchased and read the book, looking for hope for my mother, but *It's Always Something* could not provide it. I found the book so disturbing, I threw it away when I was finished with it; I didn't want it in my house. I found the story absolutely agonizing and filled with desperation. I had been seeking a glimmer of hope and I was trusting that Gilda would offer me that. But hers was a true story and it ended sadly.

While my family was learning about the treatment options for ovarian cancer, I remember quite distinctly thinking that I simply was not happy with the answers we were receiving from the medical community regarding my mom's treatment options and prognosis. It was not that I was in denial about hearing bad news surrounding this disease; I just wanted some straight and honest talk, good or bad. It seemed that everyone would look away when they spoke to my mom, my dad, my brother and me. It seemed that my mother's doctors, the medical professionals, could not force themselves to tell us the complete terrible truth about ovarian cancer and about her prognosis. There were mumbled references to "being cured", but I could not get anything definitive from the doctors.

A good friend of mine worked at the local hospital and was pals with a radiologist there, a physician who was knowledgeable and experienced in the treatment of many types of cancers. I asked if he would arrange for a meeting where I could ask the doctor some very direct questions about ovarian cancer, its treatments, how it progressed, and to try to find out the truth about my mother's future. The meeting was arranged. It seemed I had finally found someone who was willing to shoot straight with me, and I got the horrible news.

He described a very painful and fretful death. He said my mom's ovarian tumor would not be cured. He said it would grow so large that it would crowd her other internal organs. It would get so big it would choke off my mom's digestive tract. We would be forced to administer powerful pain medications, and finally the ovarian tumor would simply starve her to death. His description was vivid and turned out to be quite accurate. The doctor warned me then that my family's task was not one of securing a cure for my mom, but one of providing her a pain-free and dignified death.

Although a final, last-ditch, experimental chemo-therapy treatment with very slim chances of being effective was offered, my mother was tired and she opted instead to "die with dignity". I will never forget the night my mom called me in tears, saying that she knew modern medicine had nothing more to offer her, but that she was afraid to die. She was afraid to leave her family alone, and she was afraid that she would be forgotten. Over the next several weeks, my family reassured her that we were her lasting legacy and that she would never be forgotten. I had a friend who was a licensed psychologist and an ordained minister. This wonderful and sensitive man helped her to get reacquainted with God in a new and peaceful way. God reminded her that there was a glorious life after death, that life on Earth was merely a preparation for eternity in Heaven. A new sense of serenity surrounded my mom and she knew that her decision was correct. She knew she would not be forgotten like a wisp of smoke in the wind.

My mother's final wish was that she be allowed to pass away in her own home in Placentia, CA. My dad honored that wish and he took magnificent care of her physically, with the assistance of a local hospice group. Joel and I moved into the house during her final days to help out and to say our good-byes. The tumor progressed just as the radiologist had predicted it would. My mom passed away in the fall of 1990 with great dignity after a brave fight. While I was happy that she no longer faced the pain that cancer brought, I was terribly sad for me. This was one of the first times in my life that I had sat down and really cried, allowing myself to release tons of sorrow through tears.

The lessons were numerous through these many difficult family times. I learned to value the hours and interactions I have with those I love. I learned not to be afraid of knowing that I might be ill; in fact the earlier you know about an illness, the better off you will be. I learned that smoking cigarettes is an unnatural, addictive and deadly thing to do. I learned how to say goodbye to someone I loved very much and how to ask her to forgive me for inflicting the little daily hurts that are a part of life. My mother forgave me and asked for my forgiveness in return for the times she had hurt me. What a class act and lovely human being she was. Additional important lessons were taught to me while watching my father care for my mom when she was in her final weeks of life. My dad showed me how to forego all else to make the love of your life as physically comfortable as possible in her final hours. He placed everything else on hold to care for her, and she simply could not have been in better hands. She died surrounded by love.

During both of her battles with cancer, my mom demonstrated to me how to be smart, tenacious and tough. In fact, through the years that I was growing up and playing basketball, my Grandpa Thayer (Toby) borrowed a motivational line from an old Florida A & M football coach named Jake Gaither. Grandpa repeatedly told me, "When you're out there on the basketball court, Jerrold, you gotta be **agile, mobile and hostile!**" (I was always "Jerrold" to my grandparents.) He would tell me that before a game, after a game and every time I spoke to him on the phone. ***Agile, mobile and hostile!*** It was good advice on the basketball court, and it was good advice in life. He had instilled the same philosophy in his daughter, and it describes the manner in which she faced her battles with cancer. In high school and college I played basketball that way, and I am battling cancer today following that same great admonition. I am being as agile, mobile and hostile in my efforts to win as I know how. I am trying to fight cancer as bravely as my mother did.

Why the Patients Smell So Pleasant

"Just once I'd like to say to that doctor, 'I'm not ready for you yet. Why don't you go back in that little office and I'll be with you in a moment. And get your pants off.'"
Jerry Seinfeld

You've undoubtedly faced some kind of surgery in your life. The anticipation of having flawed, imperfect humans (as we are all flawed and imperfect in some way) cutting you open with sharp objects and fiddling with your organs and joints and tubes can be quite traumatic. It is a big black cloud hanging over your horizon that gets a little closer to you with each passing hour.

The day before my prostate operation, I went to work. Yes, I am just that exciting kind of guy. I had very openly shared my situation with everyone at the office. I

99

thought it was important to encourage the men there to be aware of the risks of prostate cancer and to encourage the women in the organization to speak with the men in their lives about the disease. The employees who labored in the cubicles surrounding my office wished me well and told me I was in their prayers. Several staff members I knew only superficially approached me to proudly announce that they were cancer survivors and that they knew I would do well through the surgery. They told me their personal stories, I think as much for their own benefit as for mine. I have learned that by continuing to talk with people about my illness, it helps me to deal with the realities just a little better. I suspect this was happening with them; at least I hoped it was. And, their stories did me a world of good. These were people who had already gone nose-to-nose with the cancer terrorist and survived. I wanted to surround myself with brave folks like these. It was very heartwarming to hear from all of these wonderful friends at that moment, and they gave me great hope and strength as I faced my own fight.

Mid-morning, I sat in a senior officers meeting with the president, the chief financial officer and the other senior vice presidents from TLC Inc. At these weekly gatherings, each of us was supposed to take a few moments to explain what was happening in our own division that might affect other parts of the organization. When it came my turn, I stood at my place adjacent to the boardroom table and nonchalantly reported, "Tomorrow I am having a guy rip out my cancerous prostate, and then I'm taking a three week vacation." I sat down. Everyone laughed at the succinctness of my report. My boss, TLC's president (Mr. Crica, the regional head of The Company With No Soul hadn't yet invaded these meetings), looked at me and said with all the sincerity he could apparently muster, "Good luck with that," then moved on to the next piece of corporate business. *Wow, what sensitivity! Thanks for all the warm wishes and prayers, boss.*

I went home from work in the early afternoon. That evening, my son Brian drove to Whittier from his place two hours to the north in Santa Barbara. He wanted to sit with Christa the following day during my operation, and he wanted to then help me, as a teetering post-operative, prostate-free patient, struggle home yet the following day. He arrived at about 9:30 that night and found me firmly entrenched in a detached pre-op, nervous haze. We talked, but I was not much of a conversationalist. While I love my wife and son dearly, I was emotionally preparing for the rather serious procedure that was coming the next morning. I felt very much the way I used to feel before an important basketball game. It was like a pre-game subconscious preparation. Hours before a game, I would find myself disassociated from the happenings around me (which is not a good thing for a

101

student who is sitting in a lot of honors classes just hours before tipoff) and visualizing the way things should go on the court. It was a natural process that allowed me to stop thinking during a game and to instead simply react to situations, because I had already visualized many of them in my mind's eye. Apparently, I was getting ready to "simply react" to surgery. All of us went right to bed, struggling to keep our minds from spinning out of control with the reality that our family was facing cancer surgery.

Whistling a light-hearted tune, I excitedly leaped out of bed early Wednesday morning and... No, wait, that wasn't me. This was surgery day, so I reluctantly pulled my butt slowly out of bed and I crawled to the bathroom. A shower was important to me because I knew it might be a couple of days before I would get another one, plus no surgical team wants to operate on a guy who smells likes he's been sleeping under a bridge. I suspected that in prepping me for the operation, the hospital's nursing staff would be shaving places that I have rarely shaved in the past (although there was that one time in Mexico back in '78) and they would be shoving tubes in places where no one has ever before shoved a tube (not in college, not in Mexico, not in any other place or time). So I was neat and clean and ready for surgery by the time I left the house.

No breakfast was allowed on operation morning. The doctors insisted that my food supply be cut off at midnight the night before. So at 11:57 p.m., I was cramming hot chili peppers and spicy bratwursts and Oreo cookies into my mouth and chewing like a madman and washing it all down with 12-year-old scotch, and then… no, I didn't do that at all. I anticipated that anything I was shoving down my throat on Tuesday night was going to be agonizingly grinding through or caustically extruding from my freshly operated-upon insides sometime on Wednesday. So, I had nothing but cups of green tea after 6 o'clock the night before surgery. I was even allowed to have one cup the morning of the operation.

Christa, Brian and I arrived at the hospital at 6:45 a.m.; surgery was scheduled for 8:45. Quickly, I was ushered into the pre-op area where the nurse asked me to take off all my clothes and to put on a surgical gown, cap and booties and to lie quietly on the gurney until she returned in a few minutes. It was 12 degrees in the place; my nipples were already harder than Chinese math. She had me nearly naked and those sterile concrete walls were not helping hold in my body heat. The Donner party had warmer conditions than this! *Hey, can somebody tell me why the hospital staff gets the down jackets and the thermal gloves and the patients have to lie here wearing tissue-paper frocks?*

103

Now, I think even delicate, slender young women look silly wearing hospital surgical gowns. I'm 6-feet, 6-inches tall and I weighed 273 pounds that morning. I tie one of those things on and I look like a damn carnival freak show in a one-size-fits-all paper cape. I can almost hear the barker along the midway now:

> *"Step right up and see the most hideous sight in all the known world. For just one thin dime, one tenth of a dollar, you can witness this 6-foot 6-inch mutant try to crawl into a one-size-fits-all paper surgical gown. You'll laugh, you'll cry, you'll be thankful you are not freakishly tall yourself. Call the neighbors and bring the kids for the strangest sideshow on earth!"*

Attention please, all hospital administrators, one size DOES NOT fit all! And I was nervous about the surgery; I could not just lie there motionless on that gurney. I had to walk, I had to go to the bathroom, I had to check on my family, and I had to keep moving to enjoy simply being alive. Up and down, up and down, I was on and off that gurney "like a fart in a skillet" (one of Toby Thayer's favorite expressions, along with "what's wrong with you, you got St. Vitus Dance?" I never knew exactly what "a fart in a skillet" meant, but the expression still makes me laugh today). And if you think for one moment that I was able to swing myself onto and off of a gurney without hanging the world's biggest, hairiest beaver shots, then think again. You should feel pity

104

for the poor families of other pre-op patients who were innocently milling around the room. They are the poor unfortunate victims who, due to no fault of their own, had to peer up the surgical gown of Sasquatch. For them, it had to be like peeking into the Black Hole of Calcutta. I am certain some of those folks needed extensive psychological counseling to help them get over their trauma and nightmares. I'm sorry, everyone. I was just following the nurse's orders to put on the gown, and I was trying to lie still.

The surgical cap is another friendly and fun-loving item that some ridiculous hospital policy forces upon you. In my experience, there are just three reasons for wearing a cap... ever: to keep the sun out of your eyes (usually at the beach or during a long hike), to keep your head warm (on a really cold day while playing in the snow) or to simply look cool (never happened to a dork like me). The concept of wearing a doily on your head to help keep hair out of your incisions is absurd. Had these people seen the rest of my body? Grizzly Adams was living inside my surgical gown. Small burrowing animals could hibernate for the winter in the hair on my back alone. There was 10 times the hair on my chest as there was on my head, since I had buzzed myself in support of the hospital's chemotherapy patients, but I don't remember being forced to strap on a paper chest cap.

Why surgical booties? To keep my feet warm? No, the silly things are not fleece-lined. To keep the hair on my toe knuckles from infecting the wounds? I hope not. There is only one reason the surgical staff slips booties onto the feet of old men with prostate problems. It's so they don't have to accidentally catch a glimpse of the world's ugliest feet. It's to avoid situations like:

Nurse: *"Anesthesia has been administered, doctor. The patient, this old guy with the defective prostate, is ready for his operation."*

Surgeon: *"Good work. Let's get this over with so I can get back to managing my off-shore investment portfolio. Scalpel! Now, we will enter the abdomen through each of these incisions and gently... Oh, my God."*

Nurse: *"What is it, doctor? Is there a problem?"*

Surgeon: *"I just got a glimpse of this old guy's feet. Have you seen those toe nails! Don't anybody else look. It's truly a terrible sight. Oh, they're hideous, and I'm going to throw up! Book him for a power pedicure and somebody file down those calluses, stat!"*

I'll bet women's pretty, dainty, freshly manicured feet go bootie-less when they're in the hospital for surgery. Hospital surgical booties just are not equal-opportunity adornments.

You've read horror stories about hospital patients who go into surgery and have the wrong organ or limb removed. Somewhere, a surgical team operated on comedian Dana Carvey's heart and bypassed the wrong artery. Well, I jokingly stated to my family that I did not want to be one of those patients whose paperwork got mixed up in the charts and then accidentally end up with my testicles sitting in a jar beside my bed in the recovery room where my diseased prostate was supposed to be. I had tremendous faith in the capabilities of the hospital staff, but you just can't be too safe these days. So, at my request, Christa had constructed a large tag that listed my name, patient number, date of birth and read, "Robotic Assisted Laparoscopic Radical Prostatectomy and Bilateral Pelvic Lymph Node Dissection – BILATERAL NERVE SPARING PROCEDURE". It looked like a gigantic, over-sized toe tag from a hospital morgue. My plan was to twist-tie the sign to my penis, so that early in the procedure the surgical staff would see it and laugh like crazy. But would they laugh? Hmmm. Or would they be offended at my cockiness and then "accidentally" make a couple of those incisions on the comedy writer's stomach just a little bit larger than normal as punishment? Or would they retaliate by strapping two tongue depressors to my tallywacker and wrap it up with a mile of white athletic tape in an operating room's veteran response of one-upmanship? I'd wake up in the recovery room, and Barry Bonds' favorite Louisville Slugger would be between my legs and pointing straight at the ceiling. I just couldn't risk it. The comedic thought was there, the effort was there and the tag was with me in the pre-op room, but my commitment to the joke fell short. My instincts told me that it would be wrong to possibly insult the operating-room staff with the sign when my pelvis was elevated into their faces and they were about to handle "the ol' beef bayonet", if you know what I mean. I admit it, I chickened out. But, dear reader, I think it would be damn funny if you did it. I have since learned from a friend of mine who is a surgical nurse that the team in operating room would have absolutely loved the joke. She tells me that surgical crews are constantly looking for ways to cut the tension in their work, and when a patient steps out of the norm the way I had planned, it is appreciated by them all.

Let's get back to pre-op. My anesthesiologist approached my bed and introduced himself. We'd not met until this moment. He said that he had practiced for many years at the University of Southern California; I hoped that he did not see the powder-blue UCLA sweatshirt that I had worn to the hospital that day. It's funny how the ideas and fears that process through your brain when you're under stress often approach the absurd. It actually passed through my mind that the rivalry between two cross-town universities might negatively affect the treatment I would receive from this doctor. And as tempted as I was to voice support of the Trojans' efforts toward winning another national football championship, desperately hoping a little ass kissing might improve my chances to get the very best treatment possible, I fought through the near delirium and successfully kept my Bruin-loving mouth shut.

The gas passer (that's what Hawkeye Pierce called the anesthesiologists in the movie *M*A*S*H*) explained the sequence of events that would soon take place. The nurse had already hooked me up with an IV, and fluids were dripping into my system. He said that soon they would administer a medication that would make me feel loopy and lightheaded. He explained that the drugs also had the effect of giving the patient amnesia. He told me that much of what I would experience that morning I simply would not remember. By this point I was nervous, so I began thinking, "Enough of the idle chit-chat, doc. I've got cancer. Bring on the heavy-duty drugs. Amnesia is good; I want to forget forever that you're a Trojan and that you're about to handle my male reproductive parts."

When he asked me if I had experienced a cold or the flu recently, I honestly reported to him that I had been fighting a cold the past few days, but that I felt it was gone. Immediately, everything in the pre-op ward came to a standstill. It was as if a warning system had been triggered; "Attention please, we are at DEFCON 5! Jerry may have a cold! I repeat, Jerry may have a cold! Stop whatever you are doing. I repeat, stop what you're doing and listen to Jerry's lungs!" Everyone in the room was alerted to the fact that a patient had recently had a cold, and by all appearances my long-scheduled operation was now in jeopardy. The doctor eyed me warily and approached me with his stethoscope out front like it was some kind of phlegm-detecting, pneumonia-searching divining rod. I assured him that my lungs were clear, and he listened and proved it to himself. I took repeated deep breaths without coughing even once. But I had made him very nervous. He said to me repeatedly, "Don't you cause me any trouble in that operating room!" I had no intention of doing anything but be a model surgical patient, which pretty much meant I just needed to lie there motionless and not die. Nobody wanted this prostate out of me more than me. I did not tell him that I had the remains of a little lingering cough, a cough that would make me and my Foley catheter unhappy for several days following surgery.

Satisfied with his findings, he called off the DEFCON alert and gave the surgery the go-ahead.

**The author and his UCLA sweatshirt on surgery day.
The look of distress is for dramatic effect only.**

Amnesia is exactly what I have regarding much of the next six or seven hours of that day. Christa and Brian gave me worried hugs and told me they would see me in a few hours. I vaguely remember being wheeled into the operating room and gawking at the da Vinci robotic surgical equipment that would be used on me. I commented on how complex and sophisticated it looked. The operating room was packed with high-tech equipment. I saw all of the monitors and paraphernalia that tell a surgeon whether his patient with the little lingering cough was still breathing. There were other fuzzy thoughts and many funny comments that went through my mind, but which would not come out of my mouth because the drugs had slowed most of those functions to a crawl. Things were happening far faster than my brain was able to process them. Then, I remember my eyes slamming shut.

My next recollection was waking up in the recovery room and asking if the surgery was done and if things had gone well. I asked to see my family. Fortunately, my testicles were not sitting in a jar beside the bed, but nestled comfortably between my thighs. And, my penis was not tightly bound to a handful of tongue depressors with athletic tape and pointing skyward like a cheap flagpole.

My wife and son had been promised regular updates during the three-hour procedure. They'd received none. So after a couple of hours that included trips to the cafeteria and much-needed catnaps, they approached the waiting room volunteer to ask about my status. They were told that I was out of surgery and already in recovery. They quickly called the long list of family and friends who'd been promised an update as soon as one was available.

Robotic-assisted laparoscopic surgery is very high-tech. The da Vinci machine that was used was the very latest in minimally invasive surgery that results in little blood loss and nearly eliminates infections. To successfully perform this operation, the surgical team has to pump the patient's elevated abdomen full of carbon dioxide gas, which provides room to maneuver the lights, cameras and tools necessary to complete the removal of the prostate. Called the Trendelenburg position, it is one where the patient is on an elevated and inclined operating table, usually at about a 45-degree angle, with his head lower than his pelvis, his abdomen up, and his feet and legs dangling over the top edge of the table. It was developed in the late 1800s by a sadistic German surgeon named Friedrich Adolf Trendelenburg. Who would have ever guessed that it was a German who dreamed up this method of torturing men just because their prostates went south?

The surgeon operating the robot sits at a console several feet away from the surgical field and looks at a three-dimensional image of the inside of the patient's abdomen. He controls the tools with hand levers and foot pedals. It is amazing technology that deals with every eventuality, except one. Apparently they haven't yet figured out how to suck out all the gas once the operation is finished. Nope, the human body gets to absorb the gas and finally expel it... uh, naturally.

Now trust me, I have farted before in my life. A lot. In fact, I have taken great pride in my ability to play the butt bugle throughout my lifetime. I could do it all; I could break wind like a champion! I have been a proverbial one-man jazz band. At one time, I had such control of my intestinal tract and sphincter muscles that I could play the entire Beatles White Album, forward and backward, in one sitting, although I always had a little difficulty completing the piccolo trumpet solo on "Penny Lane". But I had never had gas rushing out of me as I did following this surgery. I was farting like it was my job. I was passing gas like I was working on commission. These were not little tweets and toots, these were hefty deep-throated emissions originating from way inside my guts, where there was a very large and echoing chamber. When an extremely painful gas bubble would wend its way through my intestinal tract and finally leave my body, I wanted to cheer. It felt like a cause for celebration. Everybody heard it, yet I seemed to be the only one in such high spirits.

Others in the hospital apparently didn't understand and applaud this phenomenon. They scowled at me; they frowned; they avoided me. Didn't they know the joy I was feeling? Didn't they want to share in the happiness? Some folks just don't appreciate the small pleasures in life.

At this point, I would like to take just a moment to discuss with you a money-making idea that this cancer experience has given me. To understand it completely, let's agree on a just a few basic assumptions and we will use these as the basis of our impending money making venture. First, as previously reported, this surgery requires that the patient be pumped full of carbon dioxide gas, much of which remains inside the patient. Second, the best way to expel this gas is by farting; a small portion of the absorbed gas may escape through belching, but the actual percentage is so small it does not deserve more than this brief note. Third, the nursing staff wants you up and walking the hospital corridors soon after surgery; this helps to get the gas moving out of the body and gets your digestive system working.

So picture, if you will, a hospital hallway full of grumpy old men, recently minus their formerly healthy prostates, shuffling along in their hospital gowns and bathrobes, whose primary goal at that moment in their lives is to simply walk and fart. You can just imagine the billowing nearly visible bouquet wafting behind this assembly of aged male rear ends. While the gaseous clouds may in fact be highly explosive and should perhaps be actively vented from the area using high-powered industrial fans, that's not really our problem to solve here. But we can and will address the accumulating noxious odor that hovers at nose level in those hallways.

Now, I ask you (and this is where we're going to make the big money), what would happen if we were to "odorize" the gas that was initially pumped into the body to accommodate the surgery? What if each man was given a choice of his favorite aroma? One patient would choose "baby powder". The next might pick "apple cinnamon". I am sure that "potpourri" and "vanilla" and "lavender" would be among the favorites. It would be like telling the guy at the car wash what you want your car interior to smell like once they finish sprucing it up. In fact, "new car smell" should be one of our options. We'll just have the hospital admissions staff add this question to the incredible list of specifics each patient has to already note or initial or sign when they are checking into the hospital.

Picture the pleasant circumstance of a recent surgical patient walking down the hospital hallway while visitors and staff take in the spring-like fragrance of lilac leaving his butt cheeks. What a sensitive and sensible way to improve life for all of us. Children, who today have their nasal passages assaulted and run away to their parents in pain and fear, might instead shout, "Mommy, daddy, come quick to the urology ward where the old men are shuffling along. The prostate patients smell like carrot cake!" That wonderful scent will stay with the children always and will make their hospital visit one they will happily make every day. Remember, you read the idea here first. This idea is money in the bank. If any of you make a hundred million dollars, all I want is 15 percent!

This surgery was my introduction to the Foley Catheter. Many times I have visited friends and family in the hospital and seen the bag resting near the floor that was filling with urine. But I had never before experienced the catheter phenomenon. While I appreciate his efforts, I really want to meet Mr. Foley and I want to step on his throat for torturing me, for torturing all of us! The Foley Catheter is a soft rubber tube that runs from your bladder via the urethra through the end of your penis down to a bag that collects urine. It is held in place inside your body by a small inflated balloon, a balloon filled with water. When you first glance down to see this thing exiting the end of your dong, it looks like something they've pulled off a hook-and-ladder fire truck. When they're done using it on my dick, they'll attach it to a hydrant down on the corner and put out a house fire.

In daily healthy pre-surgery life, every time you cough, sneeze, laugh, adjust your position or simply think about your urinary tract, small sphincter muscles deep within you contract. They squeeze. Right there… did you feel it? Just reading about them makes those muscles tighten. They've done it all your life and that process has served you pretty well; they have kept you from constantly peeing in your pants. You can run a mile or lift 100 pounds or laugh hysterically and not pee even a dribble. Give your sphincter muscles all the credit. But now, thanks to Mr. Foley, all of a sudden when you try to pinch those muscles together, they tighten against a foreign object and you know what… that doesn't feel good at all. It's like trying to blink with a toothpick propped between your eyelids.

The name of the game suddenly becomes trying to teach those sensitive internal muscles, the ones you've been squeezing and strengthening with Kegel exercises in anticipation of this surgery, that they might never want to tighten up ever again. Once you become comfortable with the reality that you don't have to control your urine, that it's OK to just let it flow, things improve a lot. Be a newborn once again. Don't control the urge to drain the main vein; just relax and let it run.

At this moment, you may be thinking, "Yeah, Jerry, but what about crapping? By relaxing all those urine-controlling muscles, am I going to relax the muscles throughout my intestinal tract, too? Am I going to take a dump right there in your bed?" Those are actually excellent questions, but the very firm answers are "no", because anesthesia and surgery have caused your digestive system to clog up and grind to a halt like the interchange from the Hollywood Freeway to the 405 on a warm summer afternoon; there is nothing moving. You can scream and yell and rant, but you're not going to defecate. Now that I am in the book-writing business, I will be contacting the authors of the very popular children's book *Everybody Poops*. I will ask that they amend their title to *Everybody Poops, Except Right After*

Surgery. Oh, you're going to fart OK. In fact, you're going to fart like you've been living on baked beans and cauliflower all your life. But your pooper is not going to perform for quite a few days. So relax those tired muscles. Stop fighting with Mr. Foley's strange device and just go with the flow.

Of course, you'll be hauling that urine-collection bag around like the world's ugliest liquid-filled purse. In an attempt to help you appear a little more socially acceptable, the hospital folks will offer you a silly device that straps to your leg with the theory that it allows you more freedom of movement. The problem is it holds just a jigger full of liquid, so it only provides you enough time to get up and make a pb&j sandwich. Me, I gently placed the big non-mobile, multi-gallon pee collector into a grocery bag and toted that around the house everywhere I went. My homemade piss satchel worked great and was actually quite fashionable.

The nurses repeatedly warned me: "Drink at least 8 large glasses of water every day, and do not let the urine collection bag get higher than your bladder." I think if that happens gravity draws the liquid back inside you and you start to blow up like a huge urine-filled blimp that walks around the house looking like Michael Moore. God help us all if dozens of piss-filled Michael Moore lookalikes begin shuffling around town en masse farting lilac and lavender and eating peanut butter and jelly sandwiches.

119

If You Can Remember The '60s, You Didn't Do Them Right

"Don't go to your high school reunion. You know who goes to high school reunions? Idiots. Everybody you hated in high school shows up. The really cool people overdosed years ago, or they're living elsewhere under the witness protection program."
Billy Garan

I went to high school in the 1960s; it was a very strange and tumultuous time. Two friends from my high school days had a tremendously positive impact in my battle with cancer more than 40 years later. Please read on and meet them.

Sitting on the smoggy outskirts southeast of Los Angeles, the city of Whittier during the late 1960s when I was going to high school was one of the wall-to-wall communities that lived on the freeway-and-shopping-mall blacktop called Southern California. While Santa Monica and Hollywood and Beverly Hills over on the west side shifted with the winds

121

of current-day politics and the wealth of the entertainment industry, Whittier on the east side maintained a uniquely strange small-town atmosphere. People walked on the streets of the Uptown shopping district or in the parks and grocery stores and actually made eye contact. They would smile and say hello. Just east of Uptown was the campus of Whittier College, the home of the fighting Poets. The founders of the school, the benefactors who selected the Poets mascot, obviously never considered fielding a football team. Just how much fear is stricken into the heart of an opponent when they hear they're about to take on the Poets? Some teams didn't even bother to change out of their street clothes. Whittier was a very friendly town. It was as if a little hamlet from Nebraska had been airlifted and dropped into the middle of the megalopolis. Back then, when the wind blew from the south, off the dairy farms in neighboring Santa Fe Springs, it even smelled a little like Omaha.

California High School was about 10 minutes from my home in the morning when I was hustling to beat the first period bell. Despite its name, it was not a state-funded penal institution; it was a public high school. I have to confess that I do not remember Calhi being an extraordinary place to get an education. Sure, teachers worked hard to do their best to teach teenagers the things that would be useful in their lives. To this day, however, I have little use for perspective drawing, nor for any of the theories of Existentialism. Philosopher Soren Kierkegaard has played no role in my life, with the occasional exception when using the phrase "Kierkegaardian leap" (a phrase that I believe I have stolen from one of my favorite comedians, Dennis Miller) to describe some far-flung conclusion that someone had drawn and which I intended to mock. I was a very good and sickeningly obedient student, regularly summiting the academic mountaintop to receive Calhi's version of the stone tablets, the Honor Roll. The only time in my entire schooling career that I remember ever being sentenced to time in a detention room was once in junior high school when Miss Butterfield caught me running in the hallway adjacent to her room. She often stood in her doorway, peeking around the corner, like a motorcycle cop hiding behind a billboard. She sternly questioned me, intentionally waiting until the class bell rang, and then happily sent me on my way, making me late for Mrs. Ewing's home room class. Mrs. Ewing is the one who slapped me with detention, a punishment so heinous I never told my parents.

My friends and I were typical kids of the late 1960s. It was a stressful time filled with Vietnam War protests and the deaths of some friends who ended up fighting in a "conflict" there was no way to win. We listened to Whittier's home-grown favorite son Richard Nixon promise that he had a secret plan to win the Vietnam War. Although he won two elections, we never saw the magic solution, and years later he ended up resigning after members of his Republican campaign staff broke into the Democratic National Committee headquarters at Washington, D.C.'s Watergate Hotel during an election he was going to win in a landslide. Democratic Presidential frontrunner Robert F. Kennedy and activist Martin Luther King were horrifyingly assassinated two months apart in 1968. In 1970, 77 National Guardsmen fired 67 shots at unarmed Kent State students marching against the American invasion of Cambodia; four students were killed and nine were wounded. Around the country, there was a feeling of fear and of hopelessness and of helplessness. High school and college students continued to protest.

Looking back, we had a complete menu of social causes to choose from, a veritable cornucopia of concerns, a plethora of purposes. A high-schooler could select from an indubitable Movement de Jour: On Monday, the anarchy special was racial equality, which was kind of an odd twist since we had no black kids at our school; on Tuesday, the sexual revolution and the discovery of "free love" was featured, where the biggest worry was not getting knocked up or AIDS or STDs like today, but rather wondering how to keep your parents from seeing the ring of hickeys around your neck; Wednesday was "bring your latest drug experiences to school" day; then, there was "Slap Around A Russian To Support The Cold War" Thursday. Environmental Friday gave Earth Children the chance to push zero population growth and fret about air and water pollution.

While the various revolutions were taking place, I focused on honing my basketball skills, because there was a certain cheerleader who'd caught my eye. Christa and I started dating during our junior year at Calhi, 1969. After Friday night football and basketball games, she and I would quietly walk into my house, where my parents were always in bed quite early, and sit on the couch and kiss in the romantic blue-cast light of the evening news or a rerun of "Leave It To Beaver". In addition to being a beautiful young woman, I knew that Christa and her family had very high personal standards. I found this attractive, because even in high school, as dull and as "Ozzie and Harriet" as this sounds, I knew that my real personal desire was to have a family, to raise children who would be good people, and to be a contributing member of the local community. I had friends who were spending their money on clothes and cars, or screwing every girl they met, or getting loaded every weekend. All of that seemed incredibly short-sighted to me. *None of those things can be what life is really about.*

Christa's father was the varsity football coach at Whittier High School, a cross-town rival of Calhi's. Among my friends, he carried a reputation of being extremely tough on, and maybe a little unfriendly to, the boys who dated his daughters. (Christa's older sister Vicki also attended Calhi.) This reputation was completely undeserved, and over the ensuing decades my father-in-law, Vic Lopez, became one of my best friends. Vic died of leukemia before I encountered prostate cancer, and I could have used his advice and encouragement along the way. I learned a lot from him, though. Just as my mother had done a little more than a decade earlier, Vic elected to forgo a final last-ditch attempt with a horrible experimental medication and chose to die with dignity at home surrounded by his loving family. Fortunately for me, I got a chance to say good-bye to Vic and to tell him that I loved him.

Summer jobs firmed up an excellent work ethic during my high school years. In the summer between my junior and senior years in high school I worked for the now-defunct Los Angeles County Flood Control District. I don't think my employment there had anything to do with its demise, but I did find a pair of thigh-high rubber boots in the trunk of my car after my summer employment had ended. Maybe if I'd turned them back in the county would still be in sound financial condition and actively controlling its floods. I

126

would go out with a crew of primarily Mexican American workers and we would crawl down into catch basins, those large cubicles into which gutter water drains at the end of a street, and we would clean out all the mud and debris that had accumulated there. That's what they were designed to do, to keep garbage and dead cats and muck and dead dogs and baseballs and more dead cats and occasionally a loose $20 bill from flowing out to the ocean. Being young, a summer employee and the only white guy there (the men on the crew called me "wedo", which either meant *blondie* or *tall dorky geek with pimples*), I was elected to do most of the really stinky jobs. We worked hard, and I made a lot of friends on our crew that summer.

The next two summers I abandoned the putrid stench of the catch basins for the opportunity to have front door after front door slammed in my face. With another college brat, I took a truck filled with five-gallon glass bottles out to the new neighborhoods of Mission Viejo and El Toro, CA, and sold bottled water service door-to-door. These were booming communities and we made a lot of money. We ran into all kinds of people, from the paranoids who would scream through an open window, "My door is locked; go away or I'll call the police", to angry couples whose intimate love-making I had interrupted when I started ringing the doorbell, to half-naked women who'd just stepped out of the

127

shower to stand dripping wet while listening to my squeaky-voiced bottled water pitch. Talking to a mostly naked woman can raise a teenage boy's voice a full octave and his testosterone levels well into manhood. Thousands of times I had doors slammed in my face, and I got so good at accepting rejection that by the time a door crashed closed I was already off the front porch and on my way to the next house. What great training for a career writing jokes and books. If you are paralyzed by rejection, stay away from joke writing, book writing and door-to-door bottled water sales, my friends. You will crash and burn in the first five minutes.

* * *

The 1960s and 1970s were stressful social times and many friendships were made because we all had to get through it together. Two people I knew well during those decades and who would greatly influence my life years later as I dealt with cancer were JoAnn Giokaris (today she is JoAnn Hughes) and Don Watson (today he is still known as Don Watson). JoAnn was a very popular young woman. She was a student leader, got excellent grades and at the Friday night football games danced with the song and cheer leaders. She was fun, energetic and friendly. Don was a terrific athlete and student. He excelled in swimming and water polo. The three of us, along with a dozen or so others, shared close friendships through graduation day in 1970.

It was in the summer of 2004, at a backyard barbecue hosted by my friends George and Nancy Giokaris where I realized that George's sister JoAnn was not present. He said she was at home undergoing chemotherapy for colon cancer. The news stunned me. It was as if someone had smacked me on the side of the head with a hammer. The last time I had seen JoAnn she was full of vitality and was happily chattering about her life. She was a mom and a wife and a school teacher. *She couldn't be getting chemotherapy.* JoAnn's illness immediately made me aware of my ignorance about my own physical condition. I was 52 years old and believed I was in decent health, but I hadn't gotten a complete physical exam for several years.

I vowed at that moment to make an appointment the following day with my family doctor and personal friend, Randy Holmes, and to arrange for a colonoscopy. After all, my maternal grandmother had died of colon cancer, and I needed to take the intelligent steps of stopping potential problems before they became real. The following day I made the appointment, and a few days later I visited his office. While I was there, the nurse drew some blood and sent it off to the lab.

Prostate Specific Antigen (PSA) is a substance that is produced by the prostate gland. When a man has blood drawn and a PSA test is run, the test measures the levels of

129

PSA in his blood. Most men have PSA readings under four ng/m; that's four "nanograms per milliliter". Ask a man his PSA number and he'll usually say something like, "It's 0.9", proudly reporting the number like he'd studied for that score. When an elevated PSA is detected, it can mean that prostate cancer is present. But it can also indicate numerous other non-cancerous conditions. Because of the ambiguity in the PSA test results, many false-positive readings are made. When a man's PSA reading is elevated, it does not automatically indicate he has prostate cancer. The next logical step is a prostate biopsy, and many men find negative results, which means they had the invasive procedure done unnecessarily. There is a great deal of debate about the use and the validity of the PSA test. I am a big proponent of the PSA blood test and I encourage every man over the age of 40 to have the test run. If nothing else, it will provide a valid baseline reading against which to measure future readings. I suppose if I'd had the biopsy done as a result of the elevated PSA and no cancer was found, then I'd be a big PSA critic. For me, the PSA test may have saved my life; my PSA reading was 10.9.

After graduating from high school, Don Watson and I did not see each other often. The only times we really knew we would see one another were at high school class reunions. It was at our 30th class reunion that he was reacquainted with

Teri Abbott, a friend of Christa's and mine, a former cheerleader and Calhi homecoming princess from the class of 1970. Not long thereafter, Don and Teri were married. Today they live happily in Newport Beach.

A short time after Don and Teri's wedding, and a couple of years before my prostate cancer diagnosis, Don went to the doctor not feeling well. Tests revealed a tumor the size of a grapefruit growing in his abdomen. He had bladder cancer. Through several surgeries and numerous radiation treatments, Don came extraordinarily close to dying. As a man who was otherwise in good health and in tremendous physical condition, he fought his way back.

While the possibilities for recurrence of bladder cancer remain, Don Watson shared with me his personal philosophy that it would be a tremendous mistake for him to now be preoccupied with dying. Instead, he decided that he must be preoccupied with living. He found that so many people had treated him well through his ordeals, that so many friends had come out of the woodwork to offer their support, he now needed to focus his efforts on returning the favor by offering support for others. I was a lucky recipient of his generous spirit.

When Don learned that I had prostate cancer, he made it his mission to help see me through it. I was just one of several cancer patients with whom he was staying in close touch. Don would call me just to check on my emotional state. When a cancer-fighting memory or a piece of sound advice crossed his mind about steps he had taken to make his own surgery less traumatic, he would call to share his thoughts with me. He would leave messages on my answering machine and send me notes out of the blue.

Don called to say, "Jerry, get into the best physical condition you can prior to surgery. It will help you handle the trauma of surgery better, and it will speed up your recovery. And, once you're done with surgery, start exercising as soon as you can." I joined a local gym and worked off about 25 extra pounds before surgery day. And just a couple of weeks after returning home after my operation, I was back in the same gym. Everything Don shared with me was valuable and proved to be incredibly wise. I appreciated his sensitivity to my plight. I enjoyed talking with him and when he would say, "Well Jerry, it sounds like you are in a good place emotionally and I know you're going to do fine," it gave me confidence and made me feel better about my situation. Don continues to enjoy his life one day at a time and remains a close friend and personal inspiration.

I told JoAnn Giokaris Hughes shortly after I learned of my diagnosis of prostate cancer that, for whatever it was worth, the knowledge of her illness had prompted me to visit the doctor and ultimately she was responsible for me learning of my own illness. I thanked her and hugged her. As trite as it may sound, I still say "Thank you, JoAnn. You helped to save my life." Today I value my longtime friends and my friendships far more than I knew how to value them when I was in high school and college. I guess that comes with age, with maturity and with the lessons we learn in life. Today, I work at maintaining strong bonds with my family and close friends. One of the things that I have advised my own children over the years is to stay close to their immediate family and dearest friends. For when the chips are down, they are the ones who will come to your aid. And when their chips are down, it is up to you to do the same for them.

When It Gets As Big As A
Grapefruit, Lance It!!

"People who do not want to be resuscitated now have the option to wear a bracelet that says DO NOT RESUSCITATE. To me that sounds like a great gift for someone you hate. What if you put the wrong bracelet on one night? You're out having dinner and pass out, and 20 minutes later you're in the morgue. And all you wanted to do was accessorize."
Joy Behar

Coming out of anesthesia and surgery, patients have a variety of reactions. Some can tolerate all the disruption well. They wake up and carry on lucid conversations, and when the sun goes down, they go to sleep right on schedule. A lot of men actually awaken from anesthesia with full erections. That doesn't happen to you when your surgical team has just gone in and removed your prostate. In fact, when you're coming out of that surgery, you just hope you'll have an erection again *sometime* in your life. My metabolism did not like the anesthesia or the surgery.

When my wife and son saw me as I was being transferred from a gurney onto a bed in my room, they saw that my face was bloated and blotchy from the surgical procedure. Remember, to complete the operation the patient's abdomen is elevated with his pelvis higher than his head, which allows surgical access to the entry points through the skin. Between that awkward positioning and the gas that gets pumped in, the patient's internal organs get shifted around and fluids rush toward the face. My face was bloated and blotchy; as though I'd been beaten like a rented mule.

Once I was settled, the nurse asked if I wanted the anti-nausea medication that the doctor would allow me to have. As a guy who had just come out of anesthesia for cancer surgery, I felt that I had lost nearly all control of my life. I decided this was one area where I could still demonstrate that I had my hand firmly on the wheel. So the macho guy inside me decided, *I am out of surgery. I don't feel the least bit of nausea. Only a complete pussy would take those anti-nausea drugs.* "No thanks, I'm good. I don't need the anti-nausea meds," I proudly told her. As she turned around to head back to the nurses' station, the first rumblings in my guts could be felt and heard. *Wow, that didn't feel too good. I wonder what that was.* Ten minutes later I was violently barfing into the emesis basin the nurse had knowingly left on my tray table. An emesis basin is the little kidney-shaped bowl that every hospital patient gets, the one that holds a thimble-and-a-half of fluid; I quickly motioned to Brian to bring over the trash can. *No, no, not the small desk trash basket. I'm going to need the 30 gallon barrel; check the janitor's closet.* We waved the nurse back into the room, she injected the anti-barf drugs into my IV line with a little "I told you so" smirk and 15 minutes later things had settled down a bit. I continued to drift in and out of sleep for the balance of the afternoon. I would wake up, see my family, smile and try to make conversation to show my appreciation for them being there and would then fall back asleep before they could finish their replies. I slept a lot that day.

My wife and my son are wonderful, loving people who actually offered to spend the night in the hospital room with me. They were willing to sleep on a couch and in a chair just to make sure I was okay. I love them for that, but they needed a good night's sleep probably more than I did, so I sent them home and told them to get to bed early. "Tomorrow is another big day," I told them. I wanted them back at the hospital in the morning to help me escape this place, just like the doctor had sort-of promised.

Overnight, a hospital is not a restful place. You would think it would be a peaceful location for people to convalesce quietly and to sleep and to heal. Nope, the machines and IV pumps in each room were clicking and beeping and sounding alarms. The nurses burst in at all hours to take your blood pressure. And if you're like me, the nurses like to linger in the room to gaze upon your manliness. *Oh, that doesn't happen to you? Well, isn't that a shame?* The hall lights shining through my open door that night were bright enough to require high SPF sunscreen and a hat. *That reminds me of the man who got a terrible sunburn on his legs and stomach while vacationing in the tropics. He went to the local doctor and the MD prescribed Viagra. The patient asked, "I've got a sunburn; what good is a Viagra going to do?" The doctor said, "Well, it won't make your sunburn any better, but it will keep the sheets off your skin."* Of course, I'd been in an anesthesia-induced sleep for much of the day while doctors were working on my prostate gland, so my brain wasn't ready to do much at this late hour but lay awake and wonder how the hell we'd ever ended up in this position.

My 80-year-old roommate had been admitted to the hospital following complications with the second surgical re-installation of a new inflatable penile pump. We'll call him Mr. Stubby (not his real name, but his true name was just as ironically unusual and appropriate for a man getting a penile pump). Stubby had spent much of his night grunting and groaning in fitful, uncomfortable sleep. At around 3 a.m. he and I started to chat about our personal conditions. This is when I popped the question, "If this is the third penile pump

138

you've had installed, what happened to the first two?" Stubby cackled and said his first two pumps "were worn out on the ladies, heh-heh." A penile pump is one of those rubber or latex devices implanted in a man's penis that has a manual inflation method. A couple of quick squeezes on the pumping mechanism and the previously impotent man suddenly has a raging hard-on. With the flick of his wrist, he can once again get a stiffy like he is an 18-year-old at a bachelor party. It's a great invention for men who need that kind of assistance, but I kept wondering, what was the real story behind Stubby's first two penile-pump breakdowns? He was 80 years old, for crying out loud. He was not married, not good looking and he smelled like last Thursday's corned beef and cabbage. This guy was emitting an unbelievable stench, and he wasn't even a member of the post-surgery gas-passing fraternity that was roaming the halls. I suggested to the nursing crew that they deliver him a few Listerine popsicles. This guy had the sex appeal of a wet leper. I found it hard to believe that Stub's vigorous sex life resulted in him blowing through penile inner tubes like they were Formula 1 race car tires. Unfortunately, I never learned the truth, but I am willing to give him the benefit of the doubt; he just may have worn them out "on the ladies, heh-heh-heh."

The place kept hoppin' and boppin' all night long. At around 4 a.m., it sounded like the nurses had decided to bring in a Mariachi band and roast a suckling pig to loudly celebrate a colleague's birthday. The singing and cheering seemed slightly out of place at that hour of the morning. But it turned out okay as their cheering was soon drowned out by the guy running the floor polisher back and forth directly adjacent to our open door. Stubby and I had the brightest sheen outside our doorway of any location in the entire hospital. It was mirror-like. We were awfully proud.

The lingering congestion in my chest that I'd failed to warn the anesthesiologist about made itself known throughout the night, and with each cough the delicate sphincter muscles deep inside my abdomen protested the very existence of the Foley catheter's rubber tubing. I was starting to think the doctor from USC was right in sounding the DEFCON 5 alarm. Damn, so there was a reason for those rules; they weren't just trying to be pains in the ass. Do you think they already knew that coughing when you have a catheter shoved up your penis might be just a tad uncomfortable?

The sun came up the next morning, and Stubby wolfed down a scrambled egg to help heal his "wounds". The nurses kept a constant stream of ice packs on his incisions and private parts. I don't know that it was as much to keep the swelling down, which seems more than just a bit ironic, as it was just to keep his privates out of their line of sight. Come to think of it, I owe them a big thank you for that myself.

I told my nurse that I was determined to go home that day and asked what I needed to do to get that process started. She said, "You'll need to talk with the doctor, but I guarantee you're not going anywhere until you show me you can get up out of that bed and start walking." *Wait, didn't she understand that I was a helpless cancer surgery patient? Didn't she know I needed to be babied? Why was she being so mean to me?* After whining to myself for just a second or two, I realized she'd pissed me off with her little challenge. I gritted my teeth, gripped the bed rail and was quickly up and chugging down the hall, my portable pole-on-wheels holding bags of fluids going into me and bags of fluids going out of me in tow. There were other men walking there; by the way, not one of them smelled like apple cinnamon or lilac or baby powder. They all smelled the way old men smell when they have the sports section in their hands and they're headed to the bathroom. I looked around and proudly noticed that I was the only patient wearing real pajama bottoms, a real bathrobe and real slippers in the hallway. Before surgery day, Christa had altered some pajama bottoms to accommodate my catheter, avoiding the curious problem of having to thread the darned thing through the fly every time I wanted to put them on or take them off. Every other man was eyeing me with envy in their standard-issue hospital garb and cheap hospital slippers. In the world of shuffling prostate cancer patients, I was truly stylin' that morning. I could have been on the cover of "Hospital Duds Quarterly". We all commented on the brilliant luster of the floor outside my room.

Each of the six places in my abdomen where they'd made small incisions to complete the operation and which were now glued back together felt like they were going to pull apart. Additionally, every minor tug on the catheter sent an instant warning through my body that something terrible was about to be violently jerked out. But I shuffled and smiled and huffed and puffed and made sure that the floor nurse had seen me up on my feet. After a vigorous walk of at least eight minutes, I found myself back in bed with the hospital gown up around my chest and a small convention of people marveling at my incisions and my newly installed Foley torture apparatus. Mr. Stubby looked on with his disgusting syphilitic grin.

The nurses were complimenting me on the healthy condition of the places they had glued me back together the day before when one of them rather distantly and inadequately chimed, "Mr. Perisho, you're going to feel this",

142

and then plucked out a drain tube the end of which was positioned somewhere in my midsection. ***Oh my God!*** I can honestly tell you that I had never before felt anything like that. It felt like she actually pulled out a foot of my intestine. *Don't do that again lady, or I am going to drag my no-prostate body out of this bed and beat you with that worthless emesis basin!* She knew I was truly angry with the very poor way she had handled the communication, so she stayed away from me for the next few minutes. Finally, she tiptoed back over and began to share even more of her unique brand of upbeat news.

"Now, Mr. Perisho, you may have a little bleeding from the surgical site in your abdomen. The bleeding may cause a little bit of bruising around your waistline, so you will want to watch for that."

"Okay, that's fine. I can handle a little bruising around my waist. When can I go home? I took my walk down the hallway and back. Did that other nurse talk to you about it? My ride is here and we are all rather eager to leave. We'd like to get home in time for *All My Children*. Erica Kane is about to get married again, you know."

She eyed me rather warily, saying, "Bleeding might also result in some bruising or discoloration in your penis as you start to get up and walk around more and gravity pulls the blood in that direction. Your penis could actually turn black. Do you understand?"

143

Now, I am a joke writer and I am a white guy; I've been a white guy nearly all my life. So the medical feasibility of suddenly having a huge, black, blood-swollen bazooka displayed between my legs presented a wonderful world of comedy potential. I think I would have enjoyed the humor of the moment much more and may have even chimed in with a well-timed and colorfully creative joke if I had not been a patient lying in a cancer hospital beside a woman who'd just ripped my insides out. So I let all of the racial humor go in that moment of angst, with the exception of mumbling something under my breath about starring in a remake of "Mandingo".

"Yes, I understand and that is fine; my penis might turn black. Do you wheel me out of here or do I walk out?"

The nurse took a deep breath and continued, "And, in some patients, there is substantial enough bleeding at the internal surgery site that the blood begins to gather in your scrotum, and your scrotum can actually reach the size of a grapefruit." I swear to God that is exactly what she told me. I could not believe she was informing me of these details at this late date. There was a brief moment of stunned silence in the room until the angry comedian in me quickly blurted out, "Hey, now wait just a damn minute. I don't remember reading that in any of the disclosures I signed going into this operation!" The nurse politely smiled and asked me to sign

144

my one-millionth form. My rant continued, "Don't you think the chance of walking around with a grapefruit-sized blood-filled scrotum is something that should have been thoroughly discussed with me *before* today? I wouldn't have gone through with this crappy surgery if I had known of that possibility!" That is as much fun-loving repartee as I could muster at that moment. The nurse was in no mood to share in the fun. She wanted to get this over with and move on; she had other drain tubes to rip out of patients' midsections.

Stubby, my lady-loving, erection-pumping, ice-packed roommate, overhearing our entire conversation through the surprisingly non-soundproof nylon curtain that separated our beds, started chuckling and asked with his raspy smoker's voice, "Whattsa matter? You don't like black grapefruit? Heh-heh-heh!" Suddenly, I was a post-surgery cancer patient with a heckler. *Hey, Stub-Man, do I come to your pedophile hearings and harass you? Do I stand outside your rent-a-room-by-the-hour fleabag hotel and warn the pros they're going to get carpal tunnel syndrome while inflating your pecker?* I'm sure when Stubby writes his book about his hospital experiences he'll label me as a cynical, disinterested asshole; he'll be right. The nurse continued, "You can always put an ice pack on the region and it will help to hold down the swelling, which will eventually go away." She said the words "will eventually go away" with a certain lilt, a strange happiness in her voice, like I shouldn't

145

worry because my scrotum will not always be the size of an inflated basketball. Now, there is a comforting thought, *my grapefruit-sized scrotum will eventually shrink back to normal.* I wondered how long "eventually" was! All of the polar ice caps will melt... eventually. The sun is going to burn itself out...eventually. Your scrotum will return to normal... eventually.

I looked up at her, and she was all business. This would have been the perfect time for a nurse with a sense of humor to reveal that she'd purposely created a made-for-the-comedy-stage scenario that would bring some light-hearted laughter and relief to "Cancer Boy's" room. I wanted her to start cracking up and say, "Gotcha! You've been punked. We heard you were a comedy writer. We heard about the sign you almost twist-tied to your dick before your surgery. You're funny. None of that nasty stuff is going to happen to you. You're fine and your dick is fine and your scrotum is fine; it is not really going to fill with blood and expand to the size of Ted Kennedy's head. Now, get on outta here, you knucklehead! You're gonna miss *All My Children.*" Sadly, she wasn't kidding; this was one of the standard warnings she gave men who had just had their prostates surgically removed. I envisioned myself waddling around uptown Whittier nonchalantly with what looked like a beach ball in the crotch of my jeans. Passersby would holler, "Hey, Jerry,

146

how are you doing? What the hell is that thing in your pants?" People half a block away would see me and whisper to one another, "What happened to Jerry's slacks? You know, he has become a very odd person; more odd than ever before!" I just knew I was going to end up hauling around this "groin goiter" with the skin stretched tight as a helium balloon. How in the world was I going to handle this thing without bursting it? But don't worry, the black orb between my thighs would eventually subside. It just takes a little ice and a little time.

A horrified expression must have been etched across my face, because it was at that moment that Brian Christopher Perisho, my son and a closet comedy writer himself, made the declaration that reminded me we had to keep this entire experience light. It was the punch line that was sitting there begging for attention. With perfect comedic timing, Brian had waited, and waited, and waited, and then warmly reassured me, "Don't worry, Dad, if your scrotum starts to get as big as a grapefruit, we'll just lance it!" That's my boy! Thanks for the vivid mental picture, son. In that instant I envisioned myself pricking what looked like the world's largest blood blister and most of my internal organs spilling out across the table and onto the floor.

I have to confess that I did not laugh hysterically at that moment. However, I did have my act together enough to give Brian a proud nod and acknowledged that he was brave enough to deliver the joke that had to be made, and he had done it with precision. Additionally, I will readily confess that reliving the "lance it" moment today makes me laugh out loud. But it took me a couple of weeks of confirming that my scrotum was doing nothing more than just hanging there in all its non-inflated glory before the fear went away. I never had any bruising of any kind.

I made it home that day and got the chance to reflect back over the complex sequence of events that had probably saved my life. I have never heard from Mr. Stubby, but I know that he is out there somewhere making 80-year-old women who can stand the smell of his fetid breath orgasmic.

The Polish Connection

"On this week in history, in 1992 at a State function in Tokyo, George Bush vomits into the lap of the Japanese prime minister....Later, little-known White House secretary Linda Tripp advised the prime minister to hold on to the pants and not wash them."

Colin Quinn on NBC's "Saturday Night Live" Weekend Update

Nearly a week passed at home following surgery. I received dozens of wonderful phone calls from friends and co-workers, magazine salesmen and crack addicts looking for "Julio", the drug dealer who apparently owned this phone number before us. Of course, my family kept in constant contact. The great group of people who worked for me at TLC flooded my e-mail address and my mailbox with kind wishes. Members of the Lions Club, of which I'd been a member for over 30 years, sent me uplifting cards and e-mails. The messages of hope and love were awesome to receive, and I appreciated

149

them beyond my wildest dreams. The knowledge that people were thinking about me and really cared enough to write was quite touching.

I learned that simple gestures, like a quick visit from a friend or a funny card from a colleague, really lifted my spirits. It was the realization that I was important enough to remain on their radar and that they thought highly enough of me to carve some time out of their busy days to contact me that I found fulfilling.

I tried to learn how to cough and sneeze and go to the bathroom without clenching the automatic sphincter muscles that wanted to control my urine. I needed to organize a séance every time a normal bodily function was ready to occur. When I felt the need to cough or sneeze, I would dutifully light the meditation candles and chant my favorite Gregorian hymns; I especially like the ones that sound like the Beach Boys. Then, I would repeat the words in my head like Madame Starlight was placing me in a trance... *Breathe slowly and deeply. Let every muscle relax. Don't let this next sneeze squeeze your Foley Catheter. Ignore that huge foreign object running up your urethra.* It didn't work very well.

My digestive tract had ground to a halt, thanks to the anesthesia I had been given during surgery. Oh, I would win a gold medal at the California State Farting Championships, but despite the ingestion of whole grains, fresh fruits, gallons of water and a handful of stool softeners, the natural act of taking a good healthy dump just wasn't in the cards. Finally, four days after surgery I had the bowel movement to beat all bowel movements. I did not sit and quickly pinch off a loaf like every man does a couple of times a day. No, this was a spiritual moment. This was the exhilarating passage of 4 days' worth of accumulated waste material making its departure from my insides. I fully utilized all of the talent I had perfected in just relaxing those muscles and letting nature take its course. When it was finished, body cavities were emptied and life was looking up.

While I did not feel comfortable going out in public with this foreign object dangling from the end of my dipstick, I refused to just lie in bed all day. With my wife at work, it was up to me to get up every morning, shower, shave, brush my teeth, make breakfast and get in at least a little exercise. And the goal was to do all of this without ripping the Foley Torture Mechanism out of my body. So when it came time to exercise, I threw on some clothes and carried my piss pouch inside a paper grocery bag as I walked for miles around the house, around the yard and occasionally around the block. Getting my muscles working was wonderful. Getting some fresh air and some sunshine was just what the doctor ordered. Gaining strength was a great morale builder.

After fighting with Mr. Foley's contraption for six days, I went back to my surgeon, Dr. Wilson, to have it removed. Generally, I was feeling good; my digestive tract had once again started working on a fairly regular schedule and I was anxious to get the piss tube out. But I really had no idea how this would be done without a tremendous amount of discomfort. Instinct told me that dragging a foreign object through your urethra, passing by the area from which they had just extracted your prostate, was not going to be a ride at Disneyland. For some unknown reason, I was picturing the slow swallowing progress of a python that has just devoured a wild boar; slowly this huge lump passes down the length of the snake, which lies quietly as if in great pain. This is not to imply that old Jer had a python between his legs, but you draw your own conclusions. More importantly, picture the process of that huge lump passing through a narrow passage at high speed. Yikes! When asking casual questions of the nurses in the weeks leading up to surgery about how a catheter was removed, they always said, "Ah, that's no big deal. Don't even worry about it." *No thanks, I'll worry about it, if you don't mind. I'll obsess about it and I'll have nightmares about it; thank you very much.*

Bernice (not her real name), one of the more experienced urological nurses in Dr. Wilson's office, entered the examination room, introduced herself, pulled the curtain closed and detailed for me how it was all going to happen. She had developed a very succinct and accurate description of the catheter's removal. "First, I am going to inject some distilled water up the tube and into your bladder. Then, I will ask you to take a big breath and blow out while I remove the catheter. Trust me, it is going to be 'Three Seconds of Yikes', but you're going to do just fine." This wasn't her first time doing this. She'd found the perfect descriptors.

It was in fact perhaps just two seconds of yikes and it was done, and now I'll dutifully tell the next worried guy that it was no big deal. But still, I wanted to meet Dr. Mengele… er, Mr. Foley simply to shake his hand and ask if he could just try to improve on his invention. Then I'd wash my hand and be on my way.

I was thrilled. The fire hose that had been attached to my insides for nearly a week had been removed from my urethra with relatively little distress, and I had surprisingly good control of my pee. That water that she had injected up the tube and into my bladder wanted to obey the laws of gravity and exit my body, but as long as I kept those muscles clenched, it all stayed inside. It wasn't there for long and whoosh, it was gone. I knew there would be some challenges ahead and maybe even some accidents, but who cares? What man hasn't pissed on himself a few times in his life? Occasionally, even sober. The nurse issued a warning though, about the possibility of swelling that might occur at the site where my urethra had been reattached to my bladder after my prostate had been removed. She said that in about 20 percent of patients there is enough swelling to close off the urethra, making urination impossible. If that were to happen, I was instructed to hustle to the nearest hospital, explain the situation and have the Foley catheter reinserted... REINSERTED! I couldn't wait to get this thing out of me, and now there was a chance I was going to have it reinserted into my penis, up my urethra and back into my bladder. I decided that I was just not going to be one of those who suffered that misfortune, and fortunately it did not happen to me.

I felt that cancer was beginning to take up residence in my past, instead of my present and my future. That nagging question of "Am I going to make it out of this mess okay?" was beginning to subside, and I was beginning to feel a new level of hopefulness.

But then Dr. Wilson pulled Christa and me aside and put a sudden halt to the obviously premature festivities. As my grandpa Toby Thayer used to say when something bad had happened to curtail a celebration, "Look out, someone found a turd in the punch bowl." There was a problem the doctor had not seen in the operating room. Pathologists had discovered that a minute amount of cancer tissue had escaped my prostate gland and had entered one seminal vesicle, one of the ingenious little devices nature has created that help men to impregnate the female of the species. He assured us that the other seminal vesicle was clear, that all of my lymph nodes were clear and that the surgical field was clear of cancer cells. Statistically, however, this is not the news you want to hear; you want to hear that the cancer was all removed in a nice, neat package and not a single nasty cell is floating around your body. If the cancer had remained contained within my prostate, chances of ending up cancer-free 5 years from now and for the rest of my life were very good, over 99 percent. But once the cancer escaped the prostate and invaded a neighboring region, my odds of being cured become much poorer. All bets were off. I will not bore you with the statistics now (you'll read more about my thoughts on medical statistics later), but anything less than a 100 percent cure rate sucks. Let's just say that this was A LOT less than 100 percent.

This time I was pissed off. I was not merely feeling flawed, I was getting screwed. I had played the game by all the damn rules; I had chosen the surgical treatment option instead of the less traumatic radiological options, I had done all of the goofy little exercises I'd been prescribed, and I didn't run around the house with scissors in my hand. "God dammit, why can't I get a fucking break here?" I shouted at the doctor. Christa looked at me like she wanted me to remain calm and maintain a certain degree of respect for the surgeon, yet I could see that she was hurt and pissed off just like me. "I came in and had this crappy surgery done and *still* I might have cancer cells floating around? So what are my fucking options this time? Do I get to crawl under the radiation machines after all? Oh goody, I've had surgery and get to fry my insides, both," I fumed. Of course, none of this was the surgeon's fault. He just got to be the recipient of my anger and my fear. He sat calmly while I ranted. This was not his first ride at this rodeo.

We talked about radiation as a possible treatment. *Radiation? Radiate what? The god-dammed prostate gland is gone. Are we going to walk up to the machine and dial it up for "where the prostate used to be"? Or maybe we can bring the formaldehyde-filled jar carrying my damn diseased gland and put it between the cross-hairs and let the machine blast away.* Tim nodded politely until I had no more rant left in me and explained that radiating the "prostate bed", the place where escaped prostate cancer cells would most likely reside, is a procedure that some patients select. Next, he calmly told us about a clinical trial taking place at locations across the country, including at City of Hope, for which I was now qualified to participate. They were testing the effectiveness of a drug that had been proven to kill breast cancer cells and that they hoped would do the same with prostate cancer. *Oh, yippee, I'm a winner. I get to join the chemotherapy club. There's no secret handshake; there are no mottoes or fight songs; you acknowledge another club member by rubbing your bald heads together and throwing up on one another's shoes. It's the worldwide club that nobody wants to join.* He said the study was designed so that half of the participants are given hormone treatments solely, while the other half are given the hormone treatments plus 18 weeks of the experimental chemotherapy drug. Participation in the program would last two years, and post-treatment monitoring would go far beyond that. He referred me to the oncologist I would be working with, Dr. Przemyslaw Twardowski.

Recognizing that my cancer had spread and that I was going to have to go through additional treatment was a terrible blow to my spirit. It was yet another low point in the expanding and deepening Death Valley of low points I was accumulating. I was having trouble dealing with this reality, and I ignorantly put off my contact with Dr. T for several weeks. Daily exercise helped me to escape the stress of knowing that more treatments, more discomfort and more fear still lie ahead. Exercise was also a great new method of procrastination, because I was not mentally prepared to deal with being sick and weak and bald and tired from chemotherapy. I remembered my mom and countless others who had been injected with various nasty experimental venoms and how sick and weak and pitiful so many of them seemed, and for a while I didn't think I wanted anything to do with the drugs.

But a long talk with Jay Williams snapped me out of this funk. A very wise man and a prostate cancer survivor himself, he reminded me of the cancer situation he'd been presented a decade earlier. He had few people to talk with to help him make a decision; robotic surgery was not available to him and alternative treatments were few. He advised, "If it was me, I'd let them inject me with anything they thought might help. Bring it all on!" Jay looked me square in the eye and said, "I only wish I had your opportunity." He was right, and I needed the reality check. I was feeling like a victim instead of a fighter. It was time to stop whining about how unlucky I was feeling and how unfair my lot in life had become. I talked my new options over with my wife and kids, and I adopted a far healthier attitude.

* * *

I nearly waited too long to meet with Dr. Twardowski and still qualify as a participant in the clinical research program. Dr. T turned out to be yet another amazing City of Hope caregiver. Dr. Przemylsaw Twardowski, Pshemeck to his friends, as you might have guessed, is Polish. He graduated from Lublin Medical Academy in Lublin, Poland. He is a very bright man with a good sense of humor, but I

158

have never once thrown a single Polish joke at him. I'm guessing this man had heard them all and retold most of them, but more importantly, when your Polish doctor can order new highly invasive examinations any time he wants, you do not want to offend his ethnicity. Instead, you smile and congratulate him on the great sausage his people produce. Pshemeck has a slight Polish accent that I find fascinating, and regardless of his very busy schedule, he always makes time to look me straight in the eye and answer my questions. The answers have not always been what I wanted to hear. When the news was bad, he has told the truth and looked sad at having to deliver it. I have never wondered if I was dealing with anything but the straight facts when communicating with Dr. T.

The protocol of the study clearly stated that participation had to begin within four months of surgery. My operation was on December 1, 2004, and in early March I scheduled my clinical treatments to begin on March 22. Whew, I was going to make it with about a week to spare, but I did not yet know if I would be getting the experimental chemotherapy drug or just the hormone blocker. The assignment of which patients received the chemo drug Mitoxantrone and which did not was to be done by computer to assure the validity of the test results; they call it being "randomized", assigned a regimen completely by chance.

That way no human interaction can skew the results of the tests. I told Dr. T that I wanted to have the chemo drug administered, that I wanted to do whatever it took to rid myself of these cancer cells. He said there was nothing I could do to sway the random assignment. I tried to bribe him, I would have blackmailed him if I'd known any dirt about the guy, but he would not budge. So I waited to hear what the computer had in store for me, asking the doctor's scheduler Maribel, one of the sweetest people that I have ever come across in my life, to call me on my cell phone the minute she knew my assignment.

A week later, while having lunch with a group of friends before a Pac-10 basketball tournament game, Dr. T's office called on my cell phone with the news I had wanted to hear. I felt like I'd won the oncology lottery. The computer had randomly decided that I was going to get the chemotherapy drug. Amid the homeless derelicts and the business people and the tourists and the college basketball fans at Philippe's sawdust-floored restaurant in downtown Los Angeles that day, I shared my news and asked my friends to pause and toast my good luck. We each raised our glasses of beer aloft, "Here's to losing weight. Here's to losing your hair. Here's to nausea!" The way UCLA played in the tournament that year made me sick, too.

160

The formal written disclosure for the chemotherapy/hormone therapy study was 11 pages long. I read it thoroughly many times. Pieces of it jumped out at me; "We cannot and do not guarantee that you will benefit if you take part in this study. The treatment you receive may even be harmful." *Ah, now there's some reassurance!* [Author's note: In actuality, midway through my two years in the clinical trial, the study was halted because some patients who had taken the chemotherapy drug began to develop leukemia. So, for some patients the treatment may have in fact been quite harmful.] It went on to say that likely side effects of the hormone treatments included hot flashes, night sweats, fatigue, swelling of the hands and feet, breast tenderness and more. *You know, nothing says macho and manly like a little feet swelling and tenderness in your sweaty male breasts.* "Very likely" side effects of the chemotherapy were hair loss, loss of appetite, muscle weakness, nausea and vomiting, swelling of the hands and feet, and my urine color would be green. Now, I had heard of "pea green", but not green pee. I signed the documents, and we got started. *Funny, just reading and signing the disclosures made me want to puke.*

Do you remember in your high school American History class when you read about the German army in World War I unleashing a horrible chemical attack with a nasty agent called mustard gas? It was terrible stuff. It was odorless and it took about 12 hours before victims' skin began to blister and they would start to vomit, and many of them went blind. Death rates were incredibly high for soldiers who came in contact with mustard gas. Researchers found that victims of mustard gas attacks consistently had extremely low white blood cell counts. Even then, they theorized that if the chemical agents in mustard gas could interfere with the development of rapidly growing white blood cells, then perhaps they could be used to interfere with the replication of cancer cells, as well. That is how the practice of modern chemotherapy began.

Today, the definition of chemotherapy is the introduction of medication, either taken orally or administered through a needle into a vein or into a muscle, which is designed to kill cancer cells. It is a systemic treatment in that it is introduced into the bloodstream, allowing it to travel throughout the body with the intent of destroying cancer cells that may exist outside the target area or location where the cancer was initially found.

I can tell you from a personal perspective that chemotherapy is everything it is cracked up to be; it is everything you have heard and read about and watched take place in your family and friends... and more! Chemotherapy is a physical and emotional attack on your person. It is your conscious decision, because you are a willing collaborator who has signed the pertinent documents in about a hundred different places, to let people inject you with poison in hopes that death will occur at the cellular level in your own body. That seems like an insane thing to do, and it is one of the reasons I had so many emotional barriers in allowing it to happen. People participate in crazy stuff all the time that I will never do. You will never find me bungee-jumping off a South American bridge into some rocky gorge. You'll never catch me driving 120 miles per hour on a desert highway, hoping that the Highway Patrol wasn't that blur I just passed. I thought I would never poison myself, but here I was agreeing to the whole thing. Chemotherapy made me feel horrible a lot of the time. Yet I was happy that I won the coin flip to get the chemotherapeutic drugs.

Christa drove me to the hospital for treatments when she wasn't working, and Jay Williams chaperoned me the balance of the time. Around my house, we decided to take the veil of mystery off chemotherapy in the same manner we did with cancer itself when everyone started calling me "Cancer Boy". My son Brian coined the name "pimp juice" for chemotherapy. I am sure in the world of hip-hop music "pimp juice" has some bizarre meaning, but for me it was just one more way to "poke cancer in the eye". Among my small circle of friends and family, pimp juice was discussed openly and often. The drugs gave me the infamous "chemo haze" or "chemo brain" that you hear cancer patients frequently complain about. Two days after receiving each big healthy jolt of pimp juice, I felt like I was living at the bottom of a well. I had tunnel vision. I could see the light at the top and the activities and sounds of the day would travel down the well to me, but I could not view the entire world with absolute clarity. With each subsequent day, I rose a little higher in my chasm until a couple of days before my next scheduled infusion I was nearly up to the rim of the well. By then, I could view the world and actually understand what was going on. I had fairly clear conversations with people. I was able to remember their names. I was able to add entries in my journal that were meaningful and that clearly stated how I was feeling. Twenty days after a chemotherapy treatment, I was feeling pretty good. I was joking with my friends and family, I was reading some of my favorite books and I was getting some exercise. Just as I was beginning to appreciate feeling "human" again, three weeks was up and it was time to head back for more pimp juice and another plummet to the bottom of the hole.

The hormone therapy alone is known to have the effect of slowing a patient's cognition, but the combination of hormone therapy and chemotherapy made me feel like a drooling idiot. I told Dr. T that I felt like the world was going its normal 65 miles per hour, but my brain was only processing at about 40. All of my life, I had been used to participating in some pretty rapid and very pointed dialogues filled with witty and cynical repartee. Under the influence of these drugs, I not only was not blurting out my expected share of humor, I was barely able to appreciate what the cynics around me were saying. I was not able to carry on what I felt were normal conversations with people; I felt like I was barely able to sit up straight and keep my eyes from crossing. Friends would ask me questions, and I would struggle to come up with answers. I consistently paused to search for words that in normal times I had no problem retrieving. The possibility of interjecting normal snide comments was simply gone. Those around me may have felt I was not paying attention to the conversation. I felt like I was detached from everyday situations, like a third party observing the conversation from a distance, and I often sat mute. By the time my brain had processed the information that went into it and was ready to respond, it was too late; the comedic timeliness was gone; it was already next week. The moment had passed, and any comment I made seemed completely out of context. My physical reactions were slowed, as well. This made it very uncomfortable and unwise, even dangerous, for me to be driving an automobile in the few days following a treatment. I made a point of keeping myself from behind the steering wheel during those days.

Discouragingly, although I was only 53, I felt like a very old man.

Each visit to the hospital for a chemo treatment was filled with waves of anxiety, dread and fear. It was not that I was any more afraid of having cancer or of being sick from the treatments or even of dying. Instead, I felt terrible for many of the patients who surrounded me. Many of them were far sicker than me, being pushed in wheelchairs, too weak to stand. I would see the young children from the nearby pediatrics unit, some of them pre-schoolers, far too young to understand what was happening to them, bravely bundled with coats and blankets to stay warm and wearing hospital masks to keep the germs away from their compromised immune systems. I would close my eyes and pray for them. I asked God to give them the strength to handle the difficult treatments they were receiving and the ability to understand what was happening to them. I asked Him to minimize their suffering and to help them get well. I asked that the medical professionals have the tools and the wisdom to create treatments that would cure this horrible disease. Finally, I prayed for strength for the loved ones who were caring for the sick children. How terribly difficult it has to be to watch your child go through a devastating illness and painful debilitating treatments like this. Many, many times I cried and thanked God that my children were healthy and that I never had to deal with the challenges these brave parents were facing.

I was also surrounded by the elderly; people with terrible illnesses who were fighting for their lives. What brave and wonderful patients they are. This quiet waiting room, filled with men and women struggling in their own private battles, many of them staring blankly at the walls or at one another, was sad and at the same time inspiring. The sadness was in having to concede that cancer was such a terrible foe and that man does not possess all of the necessary tools to wage a fair war in each and every case. The inspiration was in the recognition that these warriors returned week after week, putting up with the pain and the sickness, in their attempts to beat the disease. They wanted to keep living and loving and having fun and contributing to society. This was the modern-day all-out battle to survive.

I have met patients and care providers from all over the country in that waiting room at City of Hope. Most of them have fear in their eyes. None of them want to be there. All of them are hoping that the latest treatments modern medicine has to offer will provide a cure and extend human life. I have a few heroes in my life, and the people bravely sitting in that hospital waiting room, not complaining or whining about what nature had thrown their way, are among them.

The hospital's procedures were quickly established for my chemotherapy sessions. It all started with a quick draw of a blood sample. I chatted with the phlebotomists, asking about their day and whether they were busy. Without exception, they would roll their eyes, as if overwhelmed, and tell me how swamped they were. They were telling me the truth. They were quick and efficient in their jobs, and they never had a chance to catch their breath. There were always sick patients anxiously waiting to have their blood drawn. We all became friends and would often recommend restaurants or shops that we knew about in different parts of Los Angeles. Experience quickly taught me which of them finished the needle-stick task so painlessly that I was amazed when it was done and I always did my best to land in her chair.

Next, I would be weighed and temperatured and blood pressured. "Oh, good; you're maintaining your weight," they would consistently reassure me, having seen many other patients wither away under the effects of their chemo treatments. I could not believe that they were concerned about me maintaining my weight. In fact, the hormone treatments were making me fat as a pig. I was quickly approaching 300 pounds. My production of testosterone had ground to a halt and I was starting to look like a fat old post-menopausal woman; not that there is anything wrong with that, ladies. I was concerned about whether they'd have a scale big enough to weigh me. I was also concerned that I was going to start getting interested in girly things like chatting endlessly with my girlfriends on the phone and shopping for cute size-13 shoes.

My blood pressure, which all of my life was in the safe and healthy range, was always high during these exams, thanks I believe to the anxiety I feel every time I go near the hospital. By the time I reached an exam room visit with the oncologist, the lab results from the blood taken just an hour earlier were in his hands. This was vitally important data that would indicate whether treatments were working or whether changes needed to be made in the protocol. My testosterone levels remained very low and my PSA number was undetectable. Had a PSA number been present, it would be a devastating indication that prostate cancer cells remained somewhere in my body and were flourishing. Dr. T and I would have an honest discussion about how I was feeling and what side effects were bothering me the most. Between visits with him, I discovered a wonderful fact about my oncologist. He answers his e-mails. Several times I had unpleasant events occur during the weeks between my trips to his examination rooms that bothered me; either I was sick to my stomach or I was unable to sleep at night or I had bad muscle aches. Every time I e-mailed a concern to him, he quickly answered and addressed the problem. That amazed me. Whether it was the doctor who personally answered or if he had assigned the task to a physician's assistant did not matter to me. My concerns were being heard and solutions were being given.

So Dr. T and I would discuss my status, he would give me a "thumbs up", and I would wander off to the treatment rooms. For me, chemotherapy sessions were always miserable experiences. Never having liked being stuck by hypodermic needles, I was filled with anxiety knowing that I would have one inserted in my veins for more than two hours. I learned that I needed to take a Xanax before any trip to the hospital. The first step in chemotherapy consisted of swallowing two anti-nausea pills, a simple action that almost immediately made me want to throw up. It didn't matter if I had just eaten a big meal or if my stomach was completely empty, putting those two pills in my mouth so they could dissolve made me want to puke. I never figured out if it was caused by the pills' odd flavor or if it was the recognition that this was the start of a procedure that would make me feel terrible, one that invariably made me want to barf. But, without fail, it was a consistent battle to get the two anti-barf pills down without spewing them across the room.

Allowing 15 minutes for the anti-nausea medications to take effect, a nurse would then hang a bag of the deep blue Mitoxantrone liquid and insert a needle into my veins. I am

170

lucky; I have been blessed with really good veins, so the nurses never had to go on a treasure hunt and poke around in my flesh to locate a good one like drunken pirates digging for a treasure chest. After a few minutes the IV drip would start. It makes a great deal of sense that the temperature of the chemotherapy medication would be room temperature, and not body temperature. This meant that as the liquid began to travel through my veins, I would feel the cool chill start at the entry point in my arm and travel throughout my body. It made me shiver and shake and feel like I had the flu, and I consistently requested warmed blankets from the nursing staff. Through six sessions of this procedure, over an 18-week period, I never learned to relax during my infusions. I tried reading; I tried listening to rock 'n' roll music with my MP3 player; I tried talking to whoever delivered me to the hospital that day, but usually they were so "creeped out" at having to sit in a hospital for two hours watching a cancer patient get his chemo drugs that they were having anxiety attacks of their own. I tried deep-breathing exercises and I tried to envision myself in my favorite place on earth (that is sitting on a covered veranda on Maui feeling the trade winds blowing the little umbrella in my tropical, alcohol-filled drink). Nothing worked. This was always an incredibly lonely time for me. Despite the very best and most well-intentioned efforts of those around me, I felt alone, physically

171

cold and emotionally terrified. It was two-plus hours of tense muscles and upset stomach and a longing to get the hell out and to go home where I could lie in my own bed, followed by two weeks of chemo haze.

I began to draw an emotional association between wanting to throw up following the chemo treatments and being anywhere near the hospital where the treatments were administered. Just being in the vicinity of the City of Hope's campus made me feel like I wanted to puke. Even today, if I am simply out for a leisurely drive, knowing that I am going to drive by the hospital on the 605 Freeway makes me want to puke. The smell of the soaps I use to wash my hands in the hospital, even years later when I go in for my quarterly checkups, makes me feel sick. Waiting in the staging area outside the waiting room makes me feel sick. But the worst thing for me, as odd as it sounds, was swallowing the anti-nausea medication right before the nurses started my IV drips. I got to the point where I simply could not do it and asked that the anti-nausea meds be given intravenously. It meant I would be in the chair for a longer period of time, but it also meant I did not have to throw up on the nurses.

The nurses who tend to patients in the infusion areas are incredible people. They somehow knew how I felt. They knew that all of us in the infusion chairs were frightened, and their reassuring comments were welcomed. I got to know them all very well. One nurse grew up in my home town of Whittier, and we discussed the changes there. Another was from Nicaragua and was excited to hear that one of my sons was about to go to school in neighboring Costa Rica and might be able to visit her country. (My son Stephen did visit Nicaragua, by the way, and said the people there were the friendliest he met in all of Central America.) The nurses were always concerned about the pain a patient was feeling and were ready to do anything they could to alleviate that discomfort.

The nurses at City of Hope were amazing, and I will never forget them. On one visit, to show our appreciation, one beautiful spring day Christa and I brought the staff a huge bucket of fresh Bing cherries. We had been warned to steer away from flowers and from candies or other unhealthy foods. It was a small gesture, and they deeply appreciated it.

* * *

The combination of chemotherapy drugs and hormone blockers made my metabolism go completely haywire. They may have caused the greatest disruption with my sleep cycles. For weeks following an infusion, I would find myself dozing fitfully during the day and then trying desperately to sleep through the night. It was only very rarely that I was able to achieve a deep and restful nighttime sleep. And, I blame (or credit) the drugs for opening up a new world of almost psychedelic dreams. A lot of people regularly dream in color at night and enjoy reporting on the shades and hues of the objects they see in their dreams. The medications I was taking for my cancer treatments introduced me to an odd new world of colorful and curiously active dreams. Every night was filled with action adventures and improbable combinations of events. I would see people in my dreams with whom I had not spoken for decades. Included in the cast of characters were high school classmates, people I had worked with decades before and, of course, family members who had been dead for a long, long time. They would be driving goofy-looking vehicles that weren't just flashy; they were kaleidoscopic and vibrant and tie-dyed. The sky wasn't blue; it was red. But it wasn't just a regular old red; it was monkey-butt red. And although sleep was rarely restful during those months, I never saw anything violent or frightening in my chemo-induced dreams. My dreams were always unusual and perplexing and a source of great conversation when people asked how I was doing.

I developed migraine headaches for the first time during the weeks that I was getting chemotherapy. I had experienced bad headaches before in my life, but nothing like the incapacitating throbbing I felt repeatedly after taking these drugs. I have never identified a trigger for these painful sessions, although I suspect red wine, which I love, to be one of the culprits. The time that I became most violently ill during these months was following a horrible migraine headache. My deepest sympathies go out to the millions of people who have dealt with headaches like these all their lives. And, thank God for the wonderful new array of medications that quickly and effectively stop migraine headaches from sending patients straight to bed.

I had six chemotherapy treatments over an 18-week period and began measuring time in weekly increments. As each week passed, I was one-eighteenth closer to being done with this part of the ordeal. With each treatment, I was 17 percent closer to being finished. My friends and family stayed in very close touch. My brother called me very regularly to see how I was feeling, even though I was never much fun to visit with. Whether chemo brain had dulled my senses, or nausea had me near the bathroom, or I had a cold washcloth plastered to my forehead to stop a migraine headache, I did not feel like I was a good conversationalist until it was nearly time for the next trip to the hospital for the next round of pimp juice. Just as I was starting to feel OK, it was time for the next treatment.

Every three weeks, a few days before the next treatment was scheduled, I began feeling almost normal. I stayed especially busy during these times, going out to dinner and to the movies with Christa. I was very fortunate that I was able to quit my job and stay home to recover from each infusion. This is something that most people are simply not able to do. I'll never forget the comforting words I heard from Mr. Crica as I left the employment of The Company With No Soul. After having generally discussed the fact that I needed to leave the firm to take care of myself through my cancer-fighting chemotherapy, Crica curtly called me late one Thursday afternoon and said, "Jerry, your next chemotherapy treatment is next Tuesday morning, right?" I confirmed that it was, as I had e-mailed him several weeks earlier. "Then, let's just go ahead and make Monday your last day." Click.

I was shocked that a career could be terminated so effortlessly. I was hurt that someone with full knowledge of what I'd been dealing with could so insensitively say goodbye like that. In reality, he had not even said goodbye; he just disconnected the call. For all he knew, I might immediately die of cancer and he'd never have to give me another thought. I left The Company With No Soul, sharing a tearful farewell with my dear friends and colleagues, and went about the business of taking care of myself and my family.

When my sixth and final chemotherapy treatment was completed, the wonderful nursing staff at City of Hope awarded me a medal. It is a simple memento, and I am guessing that everyone gets one once they have completed their chemo regimen. They could not have presented a more important acknowledgment of the culmination of a task that no one wants to face. In a surprise ceremony, the symbol was delivered with a brief round of applause and plenty of smiles from people I deeply respected. I felt like Henry Fonda in *Mister Roberts*. I had just been presented the hospital's version of the "Order of the Palm", the simple brass medal that Mister Roberts' crew presented him as he was about to be transferred to another ship, "for action against the enemy above and beyond the call of duty." For me, the enemy was cancer. As Christa drove me home from that final infusion late that afternoon, I stared at that medal and I sobbed. I could not stop myself; I was tired and I was sick and I had done it!

* * *

When I went home and looked in the mirror I was reminded that even though chemotherapy had not resulted in the loss of hair on my head, it had changed the way my hair grew in, leaving me with the most peculiar looking faux-hawk that grows into a peak along the centerline of my scalp. This look may be great for the lead singer of a heavy-metal rock band or for the middle linebacker on your favorite college football team, but for an overweight old white guy, it's just wrong. The conservative part in my hair along the left side of my head is forever gone. From now on, it looks like it's going to be close-cropped haircuts for Jerry.

177

Hormone therapy with drugs called Casodex and Zoladex continues for me as I write this book. I take medications daily and receive an injection once every three months. This treatment robs the cancer cells of the hormones on which they thrive, especially testosterone. I have heard every boob joke, every oh-you're-getting-a-girlish-figure joke and every menopausal hot-flash joke that can be told. And, I laugh. Hey, if you can't take it, you shouldn't dish it out. And, God knows I have dished out more than my share of personal attacks and jokes over the years.

The side effects of the hormone treatments have been difficult, especially having to tackle them over a two year period. Once I recognized that the Casodex/Zoladex combination was causing my sleeplessness, Dr. T prescribed some sleep medications that helped a lot. But I long for a good night's sleep where you get up feeling rested and ready to take on the world.

When I get up in the morning, I often am barely able to put my body weight on my ankles and knees. For some reason, my left ankle is particularly tender each morning and it takes some time limping around the house before the discomfort goes away. Joint and muscle pain are common side effects of the medications. When I exercise, the pain in my thighs as I pedal the exercise bike is sometimes so excruciating that I want to cry; definitely I feel like stopping

178

and heading home. But I usually stick to my guns and keep working until the pain subsides. It is exercise that I know is paying off, but it is very difficult to endure every day.

As you read this, my PSA levels remain undetectable. That's good news, indicating that there may be no prostate cancer cells in my body. But we won't know the actual status of this until months or years after I stopped taking the medications late in March of 2007. If the PSA readings remain at zero for a five-year period, then we can talk "cure". However, if those same readings begin to climb, indicating that prostate cancer cells are back at work, I will talk with my doctors about radiation therapy, about renewing the hormone therapy and initiating any other new treatments that might be developed by then.

You will remember that this entire miserable ordeal was started with the desire to get a colonoscopy because my high school friend, JoAnn Hughes, had been diagnosed with colon cancer. In February of 2006, Christa and I traveled together to City of Hope for the hospital's first his-and-hers colonoscopies. We were together in the pre-op room, and I said goodbye to her as they wheeled her off for her procedure. When I woke up in the recovery room, she was there to greet me. I am pleased to report that both examinations were clear and we were free of colon cancer.

* * *

179

When I run into people who have heard the story of my prostate cancer challenge or when I am at speaking engagements around the country, brave questioners ask how the fear of dying, how the chemotherapy, how the two years of hormone treatments and how my active effort to coach other men with prostate problems have affected my life. Those are, of course, very difficult questions to answer completely because I am still in the midst of the changes. My body is still trying to recover from the poisons I gave the medical staff permission to inject into my veins. I am still feeling the body aches and hot flashes and insomnia caused by the hormone-blocking drugs. And, most importantly, I am still trying to come to grips with my own mortality. None of it is easy. I will happily share with you the things that I know have changed in me.

Members of my immediate family, my wife, my sons, my daughter-in-law and my sons' girlfriends, and now my grandson, always held prominent spots very close to my heart. I did not think it was possible to love them more than I already loved them. Then cancer came and I realized in a startling new way how vitally important family is. Each of them was a pillar of strength for me. Each of them provided comfort and support and encouragement. They made me laugh when I was down, and they made me cry with their love. Cancer made me afraid of leaving them; not that they

180

wouldn't do well throughout their lives without me. Rather, very selfishly, I love them all so much that I did not want to be without them.

Minor conflict does not hold an important place in my life. In my pre-cancerous existence, I would occasionally allow small, incidental matters to rile me up. There was some competitiveness at TLC as there is in all companies, and every so often I would get a little excited when it was not necessary or productive. I think it is not uncommon for a cancer patient to realize that life is too short and too precious to be spending time on meaningless drivel. You'll still see me get mad, but I hold my anger for those things that deserve it.

All my life I have been a very sensitive person. This book is titled in part "A Sensitive Comedy Writer's Relationship with Cancer." I have always had compassion for the little guy and I frequently rooted for the underdog, whether at a sporting event or while watching the Emmys or anywhere people were competing, because I felt sorry for him. Through the late 1960s and into the 1970s, UCLA basketball teams under the guidance of Coach John Wooden were awesome, and nearly unbeatable. While I relished the fact that my favorite team was doing so well, I always felt pangs of pity for teams that were giving 110-percent effort, but were simply no match for better talent. My new affiliation with cancer has brought those sensitive feelings into the open. I find that I cry very easily, especially when a human being is in pain. I will often wince and turn away from a TV broadcast showing anyone suffering in a hospital emergency room. Video clips of skateboarders falling and snapping their femurs or painfully smashing their groins against a railing make me feel sick. A part of the queasiness is the result of the many injections and examinations I have received, and from the chemo-induced nausea that I have felt personally. On the other hand, part of it is the result of simply valuing human life and relating to human suffering more than I used to, and maybe more than the average viewer of these same events.

While it is true that I cry more easily, I also laugh more easily. I laugh at and enjoy humor that prior to fighting my prostate cancer I would have never thought was funny. I'll have tears rolling down my cheeks, and I'll have trouble catching my breath. The scene in the film *The 40-Year-Old Virgin*, where the hero of the film, Andy Stitzer, played by actor Steve Carell, gets a hot wax treatment to remove the dense hair from his chest may have elicited the most laughter I have experienced since having cancer. I loved that movie and encourage anyone who is sick to let laughter therapy take place with it. I also now occasionally have trouble delivering comedy lines when I am speaking to a group of people. If I am about to say something that I know is funny, I will often break out in laughter, ruining the timing of the joke. This has forced me to spend even more time rehearsing the funny parts of my presentations. I say the lines aloud over and over until I can finally deliver the humor without breaking up.

I know that I have a stronger relationship with God. I believe that He has always been with me; it is my half of our relationship that has taken on new meaning. I do not believe that God will cure me of prostate cancer if I pray for a cure. But I find great comfort in prayer. I thank God constantly for the incredible blessings I have been given in this life: my family, my friends, the opportunity to live in the community in which I live and the ability to share what I have with those in need. All of these are things I dreamed of as a young man, and they have all come to pass. I have never prayed for great wealth because I do not believe that wealthy people are happy simply because they have a lot of money. I know too many deeply unhappy wealthy people to be convinced otherwise. In my opinion, a person's happiness comes from within, and it comes from the small and selfless things we do. Members of my family have established a beautiful Christmas tradition. Instead of purchasing one another gifts that really have little meaning, we make a donation to a charity in the name of the family member we've drawn. This is one of the most fulfilling things I do at Christmas. I make it a challenge to find and research worthy charities that I think the recipient would find appealing. And I feel wonderful as I write out a couple dozen checks and send them off to places that desperately need the financial help. I believe that I am doing God's work by sharing my personal assets with those in need.

I have become a teacher. All of my married life I have marveled at Christa's abilities to work with young children. Year after year, she dedicates herself to educating them and preparing them for their lives ahead. While the thought of standing in front of a classroom of first-graders sends chills through me, the act of meeting with frightened men and women to discuss their fears and their options in dealing with cancer has proved to be a wonderful thing for me. Jay Williams made me promise that I would "pay it forward" and work with cancer patients when I was done with my treatments. I am not only following through on my promise to Jay, I am again doing God's work in comforting people who are afraid and perhaps unaware.

I appreciate the kindness of others now more than ever before. There are people in this world who are unbelievably sensitive to the plight of others. The fine folks working at the City of Hope Medical Center are, as a group, the kindest people I have ever been around. Oh, sure, there has been an occasional overworked secretary or a stern nurse whom I have come across. But this hospital is filled with people who understand that its patients are scared to death and deathly ill. They know that just a little bit of kindness will go a long way, and they deliver a lot of it.

The cancer experience has helped me to appreciate little things that we all encounter in daily life. During the first walk I took through my neighborhood about two weeks after my prostate surgery, I was amazed at the vivid green colors of the plants in neighbors' yards. I am sure that they were that same shade of green two weeks earlier, but my perspective had changed significantly. Where my family lives in Southern California, there are hummingbirds flying in our yard searching for nectar from any available flower all year long. I had never fully appreciated the magnificence of the hummingbird. Today, I appreciate them as small miracles in nature.

I deeply value the kind and supportive words of others in a way that I never did before I became so sick. Here is an example. My nephew Joshua Perisho is a senior at UCLA and planning to attend dental school. He is very busy as an outstanding student and a trombone player in the UCLA marching band. A young man who works hard during the summers to scrape together enough money to live on during the next school year, Josh was one recipient of an e-mailed appeal I sent in May of 2007. I was asking a wide range of family and friends for their donations as I raised money for a cancer walk supporting the American Cancer

Society. Called the "Relay For Life", it was a 24-hour event and I was thrilled that I felt good enough to remain at the location of the walk for the full 24 hours to help raise money. Josh sent an online gift for the cancer walk and included this message with his donation: "In honor of the best, most inspiring uncle in the world."

I was so touched by this gesture and his message that on the morning I saw it, I sent the following e-mail to him:

> Hi Josh,
> During this battle with cancer, a lot of things have made me cry. Being afraid at the initial news made me cry. Wondering if I'd die before I saw a grandchild born made me cry. Then, as I saw other cancer patients sitting in my oncologist's office, far sicker than me battle cancer, I would cry because I respected their fight and spirit so much. This has been a strange and enlightening journey. Your donation to the cancer walk and the note reading "In honor of the best, most inspiring uncle in the world" made me sit down this morning and cry. Thank you for your wonderful support and your very kind words. They mean more than I can ever tell you.
> I love you and your entire family. And, I am incredibly proud of you. Stay focused; you're going to do great things in this life.
>
> Uncle J

That afternoon, Josh replied with the following message:

> Uncle J,
> I'm glad that you found my words touching but now that I think about it I need to say more to let you know how I feel.

I want you to know how much I respect the way you have reacted to cancer. Sometimes I think about how I would react if I was faced with such a problem and I hope that I could be as strong as you. It must have been so incredibly difficult to stay positive when faced with so much adversity but I know that doing so made it easier for everyone around you to cope. I bet that keeping your spirits up quickened your recovery time too.
Whenever I experience little problems that would normally bother me but really don't matter I try to take a step back and think of what life is really about. Inevitably, I think of people like you who are forced to really take stock and decide what is important in life. Fortunately, you will get more chances to worry about the little things but I know that they won't bother you nearly as much after what you have been through. I try to have a similar spirit and outlook on life without needing cancer to teach me. Although you may be cancer free I know that your fight with cancer is not over. I know that you will provide a lot of support for friends and family that will be faced with similar circumstances. You really are an inspiration, Uncle J. I am very proud of what you have done and what you will do for others.

Love,
Josh

Again, I was moved by the loving and insightful comment that my nephew was making.

Joshua's consistent insight into my situation and the caring manner in which he stated his feelings meant the world to me. I share this exchange to let all readers know that the support of family and friends is unbelievably important in the cancer patient's recovery. Josh was one more person in my life who was not so afraid of cancer and so concerned that he might say the wrong things to a cancer patient that he felt the need to run away from the situation. Instead, he ran to it and I was the lucky recipient of his support.

I proudly walked the track that cool June morning in 2007 at the American Cancer Society's "Relay For Life", held that year at Whittier College. The first lap was a cancer survivors lap, designed to honor cancer patients and their families exclusively. I then walked many, many laps around the track at the college's football field with my wife Christa, and with my sons Brian and Stephen. Having family members there to celebrate the fact that I was well enough, strong enough, to circle that track was overpowering to me. Like so many of the other participants, we had tears in our eyes; tears of joy, tears of relief, and tears of love. My friend and fellow cancer survivor Jay Williams, also with his family, was with us as we raised money for cancer research.

I've Learned a Lesson or Two

"It is necessary for you to learn from others' mistakes. You will not live long enough to make them all yourself."
Admiral Hyman G. Rickover

Now that you have read about my battle with cancer, I want to share with you the most important lessons I have learned in hopes that I can make your travels through the medical maze a little smoother. This is the one section of the book that is not riddled with snide remarks about people and places, nor cynical comments of life and the nasty curves it has thrown at us. I offer this chapter with the clear understanding that cancer patients and their families need straight-forward talk and advice on how they should proceed through the difficulties of dealing with illness. This is my straight-forward talk. No jokes.

189

I will assume that everyone reading this will know they have to eat healthy foods. Everything we consume plays such a vital role in our health, yet fast and fatty foods are so unhealthy, yet so convenient, that we have to really work at eating right. Eat fresh fruits and vegetables every day and minimize your consumption of foods with high concentrations of animal fats, like red meats and french fries. I love a glass of red wine as much as the next guy, but you must carefully control your consumption of alcoholic beverages; drink alcohol in moderate amounts only. And, you have to get plenty of sleep. Sleep will help to keep you well and will help you to regain your health if you are ill. Beyond that, here are the 15 top things I have learned about being seriously ill and striving to get well. There is nothing magical about the number 15. I did not expand or contract the list to fit into a tidy package. These are simply the concepts that I want to share with anyone who may be facing a serious illness.

This advice is offered from the layman's perspective. I, the author, am not a medical doctor, nor am I an attorney. Consequently, I am not offering medical or legal advice. Since every patient's situation is unique, the best advice I can offer is to always be under the care of a competent medical professional.

Lessons regarding your general health

Lesson No. 1   Stop smoking right now

I have never smoked, so I am relatively sure that inhaling cigarette smoke had no effect on my developing prostate cancer. I remember my mother smoking when I was a small boy, but she knew it was a nasty, unhealthy addiction and she kicked it fairly quickly. As I conducted my research about prostate cancer and its possible treatments and learned more about cancers of all kinds, it became abundantly apparent that cigarette smoking is the direct cause of sickness and death for many, many people.

Cancer is the second-leading cause of death in this country. Lung cancer is the leading cause of cancer death, and cigarette smoking causes most of those cases. When a cigarette burns, the smoker sucks into his lungs over 4,000 chemicals with over 40 of them being known carcinogens. Men who smoke are about 23 times more likely to develop lung cancer than non-smokers, and women smokers are about 13 times more likely than non-smokers. But the bad news about smoking does not stop at the lungs. The United States Surgeon General in 2004 said that other cancers caused by smoking include cancers of the stomach, cervix, kidney and pancreas. Common sense tells us that it is very likely involved with cancers of the lips, gums, mouth, tongue and

191

skin. Add to those facts that smoking causes or worsens cases of asthma, emphysema, bronchitis, pneumonia and pulmonary diseases, and that smoking has been linked to decreased fertility in both men and women. Smoking can cause heart disease. The American Heart Association says cigarette smoking is the most important preventable cause of premature death in the United States today.

If you smoke, stop today. If those around you smoke, demand that they stop; and if they can't, protect yourself from the carcinogens in the air around them.

Lesson No. 2   **Know your personal and family medical histories**

It can be vitally important to your current health and to the medical treatment you receive that you know the medical histories of each of your parents, your brothers and sisters, your grandparents, and even your great-grandparents. If you are able to record medical information on your aunts, your uncles and your cousins, that can be very important, as well.

Find out how many people in your blood line have battled high cholesterol and/or heart disease. Many cancers are found to be genetically passed from one generation to the next. Earlier in my book, you read about my mother dying of ovarian cancer. Knowing that her aunt had died of the same disease many years earlier, I kick myself today for not putting the facts together and warning my mother of the potential dangers. Surgical removal of my mother's ovaries in a preemptive attack to stop the cancer years before it ever showed itself might have extended her life for decades and kept her from suffering the way she did. I'll never know.

In my own case, it is imperative that all three of my sons know that I have had prostate cancer and that all of their children know, as well. Statistically, it is also important that my father, my brother and my brother's sons be aware that prostate cancer exists in our family genetics and that they be checked regularly.

For wonderful assistance in creating a family history, go to this Department of Health and Human Services website: www.hhs.gov/familyhistory. Do your best to complete this information as thoroughly and as honestly as possible. Print a copy of it and have it handy. Take it with you when you go to the doctor. Don't file it away and forget about it; use it and let it help to keep you well.

Additionally, and very importantly, carry a record of the medications you are taking and a list of any allergies you have. Physicians and hospitals will invariably want to know this very essential information, and you must be prepared to report it to them accurately.

Lesson #3   Exercise daily

The outstanding advice I received from my friend Don Watson to exercise as often as possible prior to surgery and then to exercise as soon after surgery as I was able served me very well. Of course, any kind of exercise has to be approved by your doctor, so do not do anything that would hurt you and your chances of having a full recovery.

Far beyond the benefits of regularly exercising before and after a surgical procedure, you can improve your life in the following ways by making exercise a regular part of your life:

a. Studies have shown that you will live longer. Research suggests that regular exercise could help to reduce the risk of dying prematurely by 25 percent.

b. Regular exercise will help you to heal faster.

c. Regular exercise can help to reduce pain in your muscles and joints. With the medications I am taking, I have trouble some mornings with pain in my ankles and knees. So I know it can be very difficult to exercise at times. Push yourself; be disciplined in your exercise plans.

Lessons about dealing with doctors and hospitals

Lesson #4   Find your own patient advocate

I actually think that this is the most important piece of advice I have to offer in this chapter of the book. I have placed these lessons in some sort of a life experience order. If they were to be placed in the order of importance, this item would be NUMBER ONE in bold letters with flashing lights around it. This is the biggest lesson I learned in dealing with my own cancer and the best advice I can offer anyone who listens to me or reads my story. Find an advocate now, before you are sick. Find someone who will serve as your advocate when it's crunch time. And if you are well enough educated, if you are calm under pressure and if you can control your own emotions when a friend is sick, be willing to serve as an advocate for your peer.

When a doctor has told you that you have cancer, your mind will stop functioning at its normal pace. Its ability to comprehend will slow down and may even grind to a sudden halt; meanwhile everything around you continues at breakneck speed. I don't know how long that will last for you; it will depend upon you and your own abilities to recover from trauma. It is my belief that some cancer patients never fully recover emotionally from hearing the news that they have cancer. But while you are trying to rebound emotionally from that devastating news, chances are you will be making visits to see specialists and/or hospitals, and conversations will be conducted with labs and insurance companies. You should find someone you know and trust to be an advocate on your behalf. And you will be best served if this person has some medical background or experience.

A person who has just learned he has cancer is simply not able to hear and remember everything he is being told by the flood of people addressing him. If you have something seriously wrong, <u>never go to the doctor alone</u>. Your advocate will be able to take notes and ask questions that you will not be able to process at that moment. You must give your advocate your permission to speak openly on your behalf in your presence. Set your personal embarrassment and false pride aside. Your advocate must be willing to be assertive for you. He/she cannot be afraid to ask questions and to insist on answers. She must be willing to demand that details be explained until she and/or you completely understand them. This individual will then be able to share with you the very latest information concerning your condition and will be able to assist you in making informed decisions about treatment options.

The patient advocate's job that I am describing is important. It takes someone who is not afraid to confront the medical establishment and to insist on answers. But, perhaps more importantly, a strong patient advocate risks being hurt emotionally by taking on the job. If the patient is a family member or a close friend, the patient advocate's job often becomes very, very difficult, and much of the fear and trauma that the patient is feeling may in fact be shared by his advocate. While I fully acknowledge that the advocate can be hurt emotionally by doing her job, the medical rewards for the patient far outweigh the advocate's risks.

A further role for the cancer patient advocate may be to boost the patient's wavering morale. Fighting cancer is very hard work; it is exhausting. And the cancer patient will frequently find himself feeling physically spent and emotionally defeated. Couple the emotional stress with the physical demands that accompany radiation treatments and/or chemotherapy sessions, and a cancer patient may feel like he is losing hope. I know that in my case, the incidence of "chemo brain", the chemically induced haze that was the result of chemotherapy, was very discouraging. I worried that my brain would never again function at the levels it was at prior to taking the potent and nasty drugs. This is a commonly described side effect of many chemotherapy regimens. An active patient advocate can help the patient through these very difficult times by reminding the patient that the exhaustion and the impaired cognition are to be expected and that patients regularly recover from them.

197

These simple reminders and words of encouragement at just the right times will be invaluable to you, the cancer patient.

In summary, recognize that a seriously ill patient will not be functioning at 100-percent on an emotional or physical level. Find someone you trust who will look out for your best interests to be with you.

Lesson No. 5   Tell your doctor everything

You are sick, and you have sought out a trained professional to determine how to make you better. Invariably, somewhere in the mix of filling out the multitude of forms and disclosures and medical histories that are placed in front of you, you will think to yourself, "Oh, he doesn't need to know about that," or "I have already told them that once," or "I don't want anyone to know this about me" and you'll be tempted to leave off some bit of information.

Here is the point; <u>it is not your job to know what your doctor needs to know about you</u>. It is not your place to be his filtering process, randomly picking out little bits of fact that you ignorantly believe he won't need.

Tell your doctor everything about yourself and your medical condition. That is the only way he will have a complete picture of who you are and what may be going on inside.

Lesson No. 6   **Treat the medical professionals with respect**

You are entering a system that is imperfect. You will experience delays and confusion and misstatements and more delays. As a result, your already short patience will be stressed to its limits. And if you are under treatment of surgery, chemotherapy, radiation therapy or some other procedure, there is a good chance that you'll feel very tired and troubled. There is a tendency for a patient feeling this way to begin barking orders at doctors, nurses and hospital staff. You'll think it is the only way to make them understand the dire situation you're feeling.

Barking orders can do you more harm than good. Instead, you want to win the service providers over with your kindness, with your understanding. You will find that by keeping yourself calm through these periods of stress and working respectfully and firmly with the people who are treating you, the treatment you receive will be more efficient, with less tension, and will be far more beneficial to you.

Lesson No. 7   **Have your questions prepared ahead of time**

A very important indication that you understand the value of your doctor's time is to come prepared with your written questions whenever you meet with him. When you are not ready to ask questions, your doctor may find himself at a loss as to what information he should share with you. He does not know to what degree you want to know about your situation and he risks bombarding you with details that you do not understand or are unable to process. Conversely, if he tries to protect you from the flood of data and concepts that he is able to share, he risks leaving you feeling shortchanged and ill-informed. The solution is to always have a list of pertinent questions prepared to ask, to write down his responses and to keep all of your records in files that are easily retrievable. If you hear something that you do not understand, ask the doctor to explain it again. Continue doing this until you have the level of understanding with which you are comfortable.

Here are some of the questions you should be ready to ask of a primary care physician:

What have you found wrong?

What do you propose I do?

What are all of my options?

If I was your brother (sister), what would you be recommending?

Should I get a second opinion? Where would you refer me and why? (In a referral for a second opinion, you should seek out a doctor who is an objective third party. You do not want someone in the same medical group or probably even in the same building as the referring doctor.)

If your primary care doctor has referred you to a specialist to be evaluated, you have to decide if you want this stranger treating you. Call the doctor's office and ask for some time to interview him.

How did they react to your request for an interview?

How long do you have to wait for your appointment date?

How long do they keep you in the waiting room?

Do you feel comfortable with the way you're being treated?

Ask the doctor about his philosophy of patient care; does his answer make you comfortable? Does he make sense?

Is he a board-certified specialist?

If he is recommending a procedure, how many times has he done this procedure? What is his success rate? (Good, highly qualified physicians will not hesitate to share this data with you. Demand it.)

Be very conscious of a doctor's willingness, or lack thereof, to answer your questions and to share details. None of the questions shown above should create a hesitation with a good physician.

If a physician refuses to answer any of your questions, or if you are made to feel uncomfortable, it is time to find someone else. Do not place your life in the hands of someone whom your instincts are telling you not to trust.

Lesson No. 8   <u>**Know and exercise your rights**</u>

I believe that as a patient and as a human being you have some very basic rights when seeking medical treatment. None of those rights should be compromised just because you are feeling weak, ill, in pain or frightened. If you make yourself aware of these rights and insist that they be respected, you increase your chances of receiving high-quality care. Here is a list of basic rights I feel every patient deserves. You have the right to:

Be informed of the nature and purpose of any treatment or procedure that is being offered or delivered;

Be given an explanation of the treatments or procedures to be followed, and of any drugs or devices to be utilized;

Be given a description of any discomforts and risks reasonably to be expected from any treatments or procedures;

Be given an explanation of any benefits reasonably to be expected from any treatments or procedures;

Be given a disclosure of any appropriate alternative treatments or procedures and of any drugs or devices that might be advantageous to you;

Be informed of the avenues of medical treatment, if any, available to you after the treatments or procedures, if complications should arise;

Be given an opportunity to ask any questions concerning the treatments or procedures involved;

Be instructed that consent to receive any treatments or procedures may be withdrawn at any time and that you may discontinue at any time without being punished in any way;

Be given a copy of any applicable patient's bill of rights your doctor or hospital utilizes; ask for it and keep it;

Be given the opportunity to decide to consent or to not consent to the treatments or procedures without the intervention of any element of force, fraud, deceit, duress, coercion or undue influence on your decision.

Lesson No. 9   **Take the medications your doctor prescribes**

Whether it is pain medication or vitamin supplements or anti-depressants, don't be a hero and think that taking drugs makes you a weakling. It doesn't. Instead, taking the medications that your doctor makes available to you indicates that you are a smart and confident patient who is likely to get well faster.

Following the surgical removal of my prostate, I was lying in my hospital bed when the nurse approached me and asked, "Would you like the anti-nausea medication your doctor has prescribed?" I can't tell you exactly why I waved her off and said, "No thanks." I do not remember if I was still in some kind of a post-anesthesia haze or if I misunderstood her question or if I was simply in a "macho" frame of mind. But about two minutes after the nurse had offered me her anti-barf drugs, I was barfing like a madman. Throwing up when you have incisions in your abdomen that are only four hours old is something you want to avoid. I quickly got the nurse to inject the anti-nausea drugs into my IV line, and the problem soon went away.

Lessons learned about dealing with health insurance companies

There is something very basically wrong with a health care system that makes money by denying people the care they should receive. The cruel truth is that your health insurance company does not want to pay for your doctor's visits, procedures, treatments, hospital stays, medications or anything else they can weasel out of while you are sick. Every dollar they pay out to take care of you is a dollar that does not go to their bottom line and will not be there to make the stockholders happy. Insurance companies are in business to make a profit, not to humanely and generously look out for your health and wellbeing.

What this means to you is that you might be placed in a situation where you have to fight for the medical care you have a right to expect. You might end up fighting with the very company that you thought was on your side.

Lesson No. 10   Document everything

If you have cancer, you are most likely working with a physician to attack the problem. You will probably want to go on the offensive to surgically remove it, or treat it with chemicals and radiation or to actively overcome the problem in another way. With your health insurance provider, you want to think defensively. You want to do the things that will protect you from getting into trouble with them and that will provide you the very best coverage.

It is important that you have a copy of every document you turn in to your health insurance company. When you fill out the health questionnaire to provide your first day of coverage, tell the truth. List every piece of medical history you know. Tell them every medication you're

205

taking. Don't hold back; if you do, it could be cause for denial of your claims later. And keep copies of everything you hand in to the insurer. Yes, that can be a hassle; protecting yourself so often is a hassle. Just do it.

Keep a copy of your insurance plan on file in your home. And if you have someone who understands the health insurance business who can read it and explain it to you, you'll be ahead of the game. But no matter what, you must have a copy of your plan in your files at home.

Document every conversation you have with your insurance company. Keep every piece of correspondence you receive from them, as well as every letter or message you send to your insurer. Keep a log of every face-to-face or phone conversation you have with insurance company personnel. Mark the date, the time of day, who you were speaking with, that person's title and phone number and what was said by both parties. If it comes down to a real battle for health insurance benefits, you'll want to show them that you are a professional person who expects the best. And if you are able to demonstrate that you took action based upon what you were told by the insurer, you may get coverage where they are trying to deny it.

Lesson No. 11   Be prepared to battle for what is rightfully yours

Remember that your insurance company exists to make money for its stockholders. It is not in business to provide you the highest-quality health care coverage. Once you completely buy in on that reality, you will be better prepared to fight for your rights. And I want to stress here that you should only be fighting for what is rightfully yours. If your health plan does not cover cosmetic surgery, then you should not be wasting everyone's time and money by insisting that they pay for your facelift or your tummy-tuck.

You want to have every weapon available when you are fighting for what is rightfully yours. A copy of your health plan, copies of any documents you have given the insurance company, and a complete conversation log will serve you well.

Speak firmly and respectfully to those who are trying to do their jobs with your insurer. Get their names!

If you have done your best to convince lower-lever employees of your rights and expectations but have not succeeded, ask to speak to a supervisor. Get the supervisor's name and phone number so that you can call his or her direct line if the call gets accidentally dropped.

Do not be afraid to continually elevate yourself through the hierarchy of the health insurance company's

207

customer service, pre-authorization and claims personnel. Each time you are introduced to a new personality, you'll need to start a fresh explanation of your point. Go as high up the corporate food chain as they make you go. If you end up speaking with a regional vice president or even the president of the company, firmly and confidently state your position. Do not allow them to bully you or to make you feel you are doing something wrong.

Try to establish a relationship with each person you speak to. Let them know that you are a human being, not just a claim number.

If you are denied coverage by your insurance company, be prepared to exercise your rights to dispute their denial through their grievance or denial process. When my Insurer With No Heart (a major national insurer) denied my request for coverage of my surgery, the letter I received contained misspelled words and hand-written notes in the margins. It stated that I could begin a procedure through their grievance process. The unprofessional nature of the letter was my clue that I should have fought harder for my rights. The poor production of this letter indicated that it had not been seen by anyone in a position of authority and that I might have been able to get my consultation and subsequent surgery approved. I truly believe it should have been covered. While I did file a formal grievance, I did not fight hard enough to win. Had I known then what I know now, I would have scrapped and fought and yelled, demanding complete coverage.

Lessons about dealing with family, friends and co-workers

Lesson No. 12   It's OK to be selfish...for a while

If you've just been told that you have cancer, you will go into a state of shock. *This can't be happening to me. Other people get cancer, not me. What do I do next? Am I going to die?* Your abilities to concentrate on your work, your decision-making capabilities, your sense of humor, even your relationships with those closest to you will be affected. And remember that your loved ones and your friends will be dealing with their own sense of grief and worry about you.

I believe that it is okay to pamper yourself, to worry about just yourself, for a while. If you have been working your butt off, tell your employer you're going to scale back a little. Sleep in late. Read that book you've been saving. Take a little time to let the dust settle before you start making huge decisions and taking actions that are important to your future.

Also, let people do things for you. There are people who care about you who will be feeling helpless as you face a new medical challenge. They want to provide comfort and assistance. Set your ego aside. Stop being that independent free spirit. Give in to the realities that people around you want to help you. Let those around you, who really care about you, comfort you and themselves by doing tasks on your behalf. Let them make you meals; let them run to the pharmacy; let them clean the house; let them fluff your pillow. Everyone will feel better.

But be well aware that too much coddling can make you look like you consider yourself a victim, instead of a patient. Do not make yourself out as a victim. Remember, we are all going to die sometime. In one respect, we are all terminally ill. Pamper yourself through your initial emotional and physical pain, and then get on with your life, however long it may be.

Lesson No. 13   Have faith and surround yourself with happiness

While the admonition to have faith and to surround oneself with happiness sounds like simple common-sense advice for someone dealing with a devastating illness, it is not always easy to do. And as a person who has been quite introspective during his life, and even more so since being diagnosed with cancer, I must confess that this has been a challenging lesson to learn, to practice and now to espouse.

What exactly does "have faith" mean, anyway? I want you to know that there is a small fatalistic alter ego to the otherwise positive and fairly disciplined philosophies that rattle around in my head. It is a wariness or a suspicion that nearly everything that happens to us is beyond our control. It is a two-bit notion that whatever is going to happen to us is going to occur regardless of what we do to try to alter the course of events. Apparently, some very small part of me wonders if our outcomes are preordained and whether our worldly efforts are just fruitless exercises. I prefer to behave as if, and my overpowering belief is that, even with cancer in our bodies we have a large measure of control over our futures. The danger in the fatalistic line of thought is that it leads to passivity, so that the person truly believing that all of the experiences in life, including being hit with cancer, are predestined or inevitable will do nothing to fight the battle to survive. In my opinion, fatalism in the world of fighting cancer equates to defeatism, the acceptance of defeat without struggle. Don't fall into this trap.

So, beyond obtaining help from doctors and hospitals, how do we go about managing our efforts to win? Stick with me here as I try to draw an analogy. Many of you, as you fell in love with a spouse or significant other, had to learn the difficult and oftentimes very painful lesson that you could not control the other person; you couldn't control their time or their actions or their love for you. As you agonized with how to contend with your feelings, you may have had someone wisely advise you, "If you really love her, try to let her go and if she truly loves you, she'll return to you." The simple act of giving up the need to control something that cannot be controlled made you more attractive as a mate and thus increased the odds of ending up with the one you loved. In that same sense, my advice to you, the cancer patient, is this… try to let go of your angst about being sick, a very difficult thing to do. Let go of your anger at others, at yourself, at your lack of luck and at God; let go of your regrets and your doubts about the decisions you have made through your life; let go of the internal turmoil that may have taken up residence since you became ill. Let go of the fears and instead work to find peace. Just as the peace that surrounded the young lover who "let go" improved the likelihood of attracting his mate, the peace that surrounds the cancer patient who lets go of his angst, improves his odds of beating his illness and certainly increases the likelihood of living a life filled with happiness, however long it may be.

Stated differently, I am simply encouraging you to have faith. "What do you have to lose by letting go?" the booming-voiced optimist in me asks. "Believe that you will get well; it improves your chances of doing so." The optimist continues, "Trust that you are going to get well. Believe deep

212

inside your heart and soul that you are going to get well. The quality of your life, regardless of how long that is, will be improved. Live a happy life; what do you have to lose?" The optimist in me continues to win the internal debate, and I encourage you to have faith, to be upbeat, and to stay positive.

I am a Christian who believes that Jesus Christ is the Son of God. I believe in God Himself and in Heaven. I pray to God every day and thank him for the unbelievably happy life I am living. While encouraging the religious reader to pray for strength and wisdom and healing and to offer thanks, the faith I am encouraging you to maintain during your illness transcends any one single set of religious doctrines. I am urging you to hold on to a strong, unwavering internally-centered commitment that you can beat your illness. Maintain the belief that you can win because the unwavering positive belief that you will defeat cancer increases your chances of getting well.

Finally, I want to encourage you to surround yourself with happy things; it, too, will increase your chances of winning. Open the blinds and let the sun shine in. There is life to be lived, and I want you to enjoy it to the fullest. Take a walk on the beach at sunset and breathe in the moist ocean air. Stroll calmly in the mountains or the desert or just down the street. Take some time to revisit the happiest memories of your life. And take some time to quietly evaluate your situation. Frankly, today if I lived anywhere near Oskaloosa, Iowa, I would rent a small motorboat and go fishing for catfish and carp on the Des Moines River, like I did with my Grandpa 45 years ago. Reliving those memories would do me good. I would love to crack open the jar of "stink bait" and anticipate that horrible stench that attracts the catfish. I would love to hear the water lap up against the sides of the aluminum boat. I would love to hear the steady purr of a distant outboard motor. If you enjoy music, put the classics or big bands or country on your CD player and listen to it for hours on end. Escape and feel good. Cuddle up with the dog or just watch the fish peacefully meander around the tank. It's soothing and it's therapeutic and it's good for you.

Something that is just as important as focusing on the positive aspects of your life is making the conscious effort to steer clear of the negative influences that swirl all around you. Don't let them near you, not physically, emotionally, nor spiritually. Don't let the naysayers have any power in your battle with cancer. Don't listen to them. Don't let them drag you down. Don't let them make you doubt that you can win. Don't let them sap your physical or emotional energy. I can tell you from personal experience that many of the losers in your life will automatically stay away from you once they hear you are sick. Anyone with cancer scares them to death and

214

they're so shallow that their friendships were probably meaningless to start with. Many of them live lives that are based on shallow outward appearances, and your illness just doesn't fit into the pretty picture they are trying to portray. Yes, one day they will be forced to face the difficult realities that you are facing today. Perhaps you will be able to tend to their needs in a way they were unable to tend to yours. For now, allow them, even encourage them, to stay away from you.

Have faith and surround yourself with the things and the people who bring joy to your life.

Lesson No. 14   **Keep and cultivate your sense of humor**

We each have our brand of humor that is a part of our psychological makeup. What makes me laugh out loud might only bring a smile to your face and vice versa. It is important that each of us identifies the types of humor that make us laugh and acknowledge them.

Then create a library of books and videos and other references filled with examples of the types of humor that you love. Build that library and refer to it frequently. The laughter that you enjoy will help to reduce the physical pain, it will help to reduce the stresses you are feeling, and it will help to remind you that there is more to life than illness and treatments and fear. My strong belief is that your laughter will help you to fight your illness. It is not the cure-all to dealing with cancer or any other medical challenge, but it is truly one of the weapons you want to have in your arsenal.

A Special Comment About Dealing with Medical Statistics

Scottish journalist and poet Andrew Lang said, "An unsophisticated forecaster uses statistics as a drunken man uses lampposts -- for support rather than for illumination." He was right. And the unsophisticated reader of statistics, or perhaps the emotionally injured patient who has recently learned he has cancer, is at risk of reading raw data and allowing it to unfairly and negatively affect his actions in fighting his illness.

The emotional rollercoaster ride known as a cancer diagnosis can be miserable. Starting the day you learn you have the disease, you will have highs and lows imposed upon you by the information you hear from doctors, hospitals, pathology labs and insurance companies. It often seems that much of your emotional journey is running wildly outside of your control. You, the new patient, might encounter bulging reams of historical data regarding people who have dealt with your illness and that reveal their outcomes.

216

When I learned after surgery that my prostate cancer had spread to one of my seminal vesicles, I was angry and I yelled at my surgeon. I was afraid of having to deal with more treatments and based on the statistics I was being shown I was afraid of dying. The historical data said that my chances of being cured were rather dramatically diminished. Being just the common man, those fears paralyzed me almost long enough that one of my best treatment options would have been no longer available. It took me at least a month to completely snap out of it and to once again begin acting in my own best interests.

In this entire book, this is the section that will please the medical community the least. Physicians do not want their patients to hear the message, "Ignore the negative data." And although that is not precisely what I am encouraging anyone to do, that is the way many will read it. All that I am really encouraging anyone to do in the following paragraphs is to keep the statistical data about cancer in their proper place. Do not let the historical data about your disease, whether it is positive or negative, force you to fit neatly into what you might believe is a predetermined expectation or outcome.

If you have been diagnosed with cancer, you'll quickly realize you hate all of the statistical reporting related to the disease. Your doctors, along with your own research, will tell you about how many hundreds of thousands of people will be treated each year for your form of the disease. You'll hear about five-year survival rates and death rates and recurrence rates and cure rates. The overwhelming wave of data can be very depressing, even when the numbers support the potential for you being cured. Since even the most optimistic situations usually have at least a few people who die, every circumstance presents a risk, and I believe the average human mind tends to gravitate toward the worst-case scenarios. Regardless of how hard you search, nowhere is it going to say, "You're going get well, for sure; guaranteed." This lack of total reassurance is a trap, my friends, created by the nasty little negative doubts that hide in the backs of our minds. Don't let the lack of 100-percent assurances keep you from fighting at 100-percent of your capabilities.

When Benjamin Disraeli, and later Mark Twain, said, "There are three kinds of lies: lies, damn lies and statistics," they were not talking about the vitally important statistical information being shared with you by your doctors. They and the medical world are not lying to you about the data. They have a moral obligation to share the historical facts with you. But your mind may be unclear or completely wrong in the conclusions it draws from the data that your doctor and you are feeding it.

The source of much of the fear rushing through the patient's brain, the cause of the emotional trauma, is the dreaded "Bell Curve". It is the same damned bell curve that was responsible for every "D" you ever got on a test paper in junior high school, even though you got 84 percent of the questions right. Taking the easy route, your teacher would decide that it was wise to give just as many students "F's" as would get "A's". A few more students would get "B's" and "D's". And, more of the class got "C's" than any other grade. It's the bell curve; the standard normal distribution of results and a mainstay in the calculated world of statisticians.

The same bell curve is encountered in myriad occurrences throughout your life, including the treatment of cancer and the determination of cure rates. The same distribution curve exists. It looks like this:

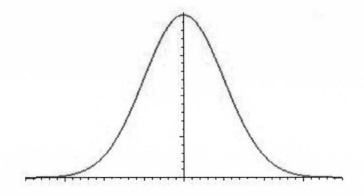

Because I hate this thing so much, I'll be brief in my explanation of its principles. The data along the horizontal axis represents time. It can be measured in days, months, years, maybe even decades. For the argument I am making in this section, the exact time frames do not matter. The vertical axis represents numbers of patients. Briefly, the bell curve says that a few patients with your disease (and my disease and every other disease) will overcome their illness and live a long time; those are the patients who would fall into the far right side of the curve. The few patients who would die quickly are represented in those at the far left-hand edge of the curve. The vast majority of patients fall into the middle section of the curve along the "mean line". That indicates the average length of survival. You can look, but you will not find your name or my name anywhere on that bell curve. That's the beauty of this analysis. You are not old data; you are alive and fighting and not represented in the historical data you'll be shown.

Here is my battle cry regarding the statistics used in cancer-cure predictions: ***Screw the bell curve***! That's right, let's all survive and totally screw with the mathematician's nasty tool that tells him when we're expected to die! He is not God, and his depressing printouts do not have to foretell your destiny.

I believe that by diagnosing our illnesses earlier than ever before, by being better educated about our illnesses than ever before, by treating our illnesses more aggressively and intelligently than ever before, which includes using the latest treatments, techniques and medications, we can change this graph. We can skew it in favor of survival. It may have the same lousy bell shape, but we can move it dramatically to the right and show the world that cancer patients are living longer; that we are being cured in astonishingly large numbers. Actually, the numbers show that we already are living longer today than in the past. In the 10 most commonly diagnosed cancers, almost without exception, five-year survival rates are increasing and mortality rates are decreasing. We are moving the bell curve to the right, like this:

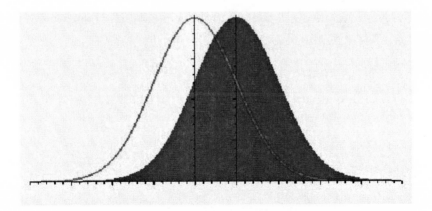

We are "living in the shaded area" in greater and greater numbers. Use this reality as encouragement to fight, to battle and to win.

Please do not be disheartened by any negative historical data you see in the literature you will receive from your doctor or that you find in your own research. Remember these things:

1. There *are* people with *your* type of cancer who "live" on the far right edges of that bell curve; they did survive and thrive and are living for a long, long time. You might be one of them;

2. There are people with your type of cancer in the statistical array who were so paralyzed by their diagnosis that they elected to do nothing or simply did not have resources available to wage an expensive battle; many of them are represented in the far left-hand portion of the curve (the short survival-period portion); they have skewed the curve to the left by being part of the data represented there; and

3. With the new medications and treatments, and the healthier attitudes we all have toward cancer and your positive efforts to survive, you do not have to be a mere statistic with your place on the traditional bell-curve timeline predetermined.

Make a commitment to yourself; make a commitment to me. Let's commit to staying aggressive in our battles against cancer and to adopting the most positive attitudes we can. Recognize that by enjoying every minute we have on the earth, we improve our chances of getting well. Finally, make the promise that you'll do everything possible to screw up the bell curve and show the statisticians we're not willing to fit neatly into their data-driven predictions.

Epilogue

I have very sad news to report regarding my dear friend JoAnn Hughes. Repeatedly, she fought relapses of her colon cancer. Even though she was sick, she traveled through Europe with family and enjoyed every minute of her remaining life. I am saddened to tell you that my friend died of colon cancer in December of 2007. JoAnn, you are one of my heroes!

The other high school friend you met earlier, Don Watson, is doing well. He is coaching water polo at the high school level and, with his bride Teri, is enjoying every moment of his life.

Another invaluable friend who is fighting cancer, Jay Williams, is now aggressively using hormone therapy to keep his PSA number under control. Prostate cancer cells in his body are reacting appropriately to the new treatments and I am pleased to report that Jay's PSA levels have plummeted.

In my own life, I have little but good news to report. Throughout this book, I have caustically implied that men who have their prostates removed face an erection-free life complicated with the inability to control their pee. Surgeons' new nerve-sparing prostate-removal techniques have resulted in me regaining the ability to have erections and in truth I have had little trouble with urinary control from the time my catheter was removed about one week after my surgery.

Appendix

There is an entire world of information available to you about the type of cancer you have. While the massive quantities of literature coming at you can be daunting, it is far better to begin to wade through it and determine a direction than to be so overwhelmed by it that you become paralyzed. Time is precious, and actively addressing your situation can help add years to your life.

Listed below are websites of organizations that can be trusted, organizations that can inform you and help you to create an action plan. Start by logging on to just one site.

227

Get some basic information about your illness. Follow the paths they make available to you.

Each of the organizations listed below has a link on my website, www.jerryperisho.com. Go there and click your way to each of the following sites to begin gathering information.

<u>Organizations and their Websites</u>

American Cancer Society at www.cancer.org

National Cancer Institute at www.cancer.gov

Centers for Disease Control at www.cdc.gov

Lance Armstrong Foundation at www.livestrong.org

MedicineNet.com

North American Association of Central Cancer
Registries at www.naaccr.org

Cancer Prevention Newsletter at
www.nypcancerprevention.com

American Society of Clinical Oncology at
www.asco.org

National Institutes of Health at www.nih.gov

<u>For prostate cancer specifically</u>

Prostate Cancer Foundation at
www.prostatecancerfoundation.org

Prostate Cancer Research Institute at

www.prostate-cancer.org

Prostate Institute of America at www.pioa.org

Prostate Pointers at www.prostatepointers.org

Johns Hopkins Prostate Bulletin at

www.hopkinsprostate.com

Us TOO Prostate Cancer Education and Support at

www.ustoo.com

Hospitals

Association of Community Cancer Centers at

www.accc-cancer.org

City of Hope at www.cityofhope.org

To arrange for media interviews, personal appearances or special contact with the author, visit www.jerryperisho.com or send an e-mail to one of the following addresses:

jerryperisho@earthlink.net

or

jerryperisho@gmail.com

If you are requesting more copies of

I Barf, Therefore I Am

By Jerry Perisho

please visit

www.jerryperisho.com

or send an email to

jerryperisho@earthlink.net

or

jerryperisho@gmail.com